SECRETARIA
CASE STUDIES

John Harrison and Marion Leishman

Pitman

PITMAN PUBLISHING
128 Long Acre, London WC2E 9AN
A Division of Longman Group UK Limited

© John Harrison and Marion Leishman 1989

First published in Great Britain 1989

British Library Cataloguing in Publication Data
Harrison, John
  Secretarial case studies
  1. Secretaryship
  I. Title II. Leishman, Marion
  651.3'741

ISBN 0-273-03001-9

Printed and bound in Singapore

Contents

Preface   iv
The case study approach to learning   vi
Acknowledgements   viii

Case studies:

1   Carter, Parker & Watts, chartered accountants   1
2   Television Vectis   7
3   Pitman Publishing   14
4   Esso UK plc   25
5   Manville Limited, builders   34
6   IBM UK Limited   45
7   The Industrial Society   53
8   Abraham & Fothergil, solicitors   62
9   Barratts – The House Builders   70
10   A local branch of the Midland Bank   77
11   Warner-Lambert (UK) Limited   86
12   University College Hospital and Middlesex School of
        Medicine   97
13   Southampton University   105
14   Montagu Car Museum   113
15   Tate & Lyle PLC   123
16   Draper Tools Limited   129
17   *Prima* magazine   136
18   Peter Green – household and contract furnishers   145
19   Southampton City Council   154
20   Jobways Commercial Services   168

Comparisons and conclusions   175
Index of topics in the activities   178

Preface

During our interviews with secretaries for the case studies in this book we were made aware of the prestigious and demanding role they now occupy, especially in the work involved in organising the office and extracting the information which their employers require to make decisions and formulate policies. With the aid of modern word processors, secretaries spend less time producing typewritten work and more time in an active administrative capacity for their companies, making full use of their initiative and office management skills. From our relatively small sample of secretarial positions we are more than ever convinced that the secretary occupies a key position in the management team and should continue to do so with the increasing use of new technology and the need for efficiency in the office.

We would wish to reiterate our thanks to all the secretaries we were privileged to interview for these case studies. They were all most helpful and considerate, especially when we asked them to tell us about their problems and difficult situations. We also wish to thank their employers for their co-operation and for allowing us to intrude into the privacy of their offices and spend an hour or two with their secretaries.

All of the case studies are contributed by private secretaries and personal assistants at work and are, therefore, drawn from current business administrative practices, reflecting as they do the secretarial scenarios and problems in everyday office situations. We have included a cross-section of organisations differing greatly in style, aims and size, and drawn from both the private and public sectors, involving manufacturing, the service industries and the professions.

Each case study contains:

- background information about the organisation
- an organisation chart
- a study of a specific personnel role
- problems and situations associated with secretarial and administrative services
- a page of student activities

The activities are grouped under the subject headings:

- Secretarial procedures (intermediate)
- Secretarial administration (advanced)

- Structure of business
- Management appreciation

By bringing these subject areas together we hope that it will provide the opportunity for an integrated teaching approach.

The case studies are comprehensive and provide a realistic setting for the activities but they do not supply all of the answers. Students should be encouraged to develop their own ideas and find out information for themselves by turning to their textbooks, reference books, journals and other sources and, as a result, 'learn by doing'.

The questions relate very closely to those set in the London Chamber of Commerce Private and Executive Secretary's Diploma and Private Secretary's Certificate, and the secretarial examinations of the Royal Society of Arts (such as the Higher Diploma in Administrative Procedures), Pitman Examinations Institute and the Business and Technician Education Council.

The tasks are designed as the basis for assignments, examinations, class discussions and role-playing exercises and lecturers can also use the case studies and organisation charts to develop any other aspects of the organisations to suit their own assignment plans.

As well as providing a series of case studies for learning activities in administrative and secretarial courses, the book will be of interest to those who require up-to-date information about careers and opportunities available for secretaries and administrative staff.

We hope that our readers will enjoy the insight we have provided into the twenty organisations as much as we have enjoyed our enquiries and that, by completing the activities, they will develop the necessary skills to be successful in employment.

ML/JH

The material on which these case studies are based was supplied at the time of the authors' research and does not take account of any changes that may have taken place subsequently in the organisations referred to.

The case study approach to learning

In writing these case studies, based on current business organisations, the authors have considered the needs of both lecturers and students. The backgrounds given provide an introduction to the development of companies, public authorities, etc, and their progress to date.

FROM THE STUDENT'S POINT OF VIEW

Firstly, the student needs to be introduced to the business world and the assignments given in this book will assist in developing such knowledge and skills. By providing an historical background, the reader is taken into the offices of a range of organisations, large and small, private and public, and acquainted with their personnel.

A section of each case study is viewed through the eyes of a member of the staff, usually a secretary, and the student can identify with that person. A problem-solving page is provided to develop skills of recall, research, analysis, use of initiative and an understanding of modern administrative practices. The situations enable the student to learn through association with an organisation, and it is hoped that this experience will be both enjoyable and thought-provoking.

FROM THE LECTURER'S POINT OF VIEW

The authors have provided a teaching tool which can be used to develop problem-solving skills. Alternatively, individual needs can be satisfied with lecturers using the company details, organisation charts and departmental roles to develop their own assignments for any additional skills, knowledge and interests required.

SPECIFIC SKILLS DEVELOPED THROUGH THE CASE STUDY APPROACH

- An awareness of the differences in company structures and personnel. Within companies, whether large or small, many of the administrative problems are similar even if they are on a varied scale
- The development of decision-making skills. The questions set aim to foster the ability to make personal judgements that may differ within a group and prompt further discussion
- Interpersonal and communication skills. It is hoped that group work will reveal different approaches and solutions to the same problem
- Working together as a team in the 'role play' and 'find out' activities. Opportunities are given for students to observe and use interpersonal and communication skills. The framework of case studies allows flexibility for the material to be used in other ways
- Preparation for examinations and assessed assignments. Not only do students gain an insight into nationally-known organisations and smaller firms (probably existing in their locality under different names) but also the questions are based on past examination papers and are considered relevant in present-day employment
- Integration of subjects to achieve an overall appreciation of tasks and their solutions
- An insight into the wide range of secretarial careers available in industry, commerce and public authorities
- Development of information gathering skills

GUIDELINES FOR STUDENTS

How to approach each case study:
- Read the background notes carefully
- Study the organisation chart
- Familiarise yourself with the work carried out by the staff depicted in the organisation
- Relate your answers to the questions to the background of the case study, constantly referring back to the circumstances of a particular organisation
- Identify and analyse the situation given in an activity:

    What is the problem? (underline key words)

              are you trying to achieve? (study the requirements of the question)

              facts do you need? (make a list)

              format is required? (report, memo, letter, oral presentation, etc)

    Why has the problem arisen? (re-read the background)

Where can you obtain the information? (make use of your local library, newspapers, etc)

When must the assignment be completed? (note the date in your diary)

How are you going to organise your time to complete the work? (schedule your work activities carefully to ensure that you meet the deadline set)

- Review your work, proofreading it to correct mistakes or omissions
- Seek advice or help from peers, lecturers, work colleagues or other experts when necessary
- When your work is returned to you after assessment learn from your mistakes and omissions, accept criticism and, if necessary, be prepared to modify your views – your aim being to progress to competent levels of achievement
- Use the 'find out' and 'role play' activities to develop your knowledge and an ability to express your views and conduct your enquiries in an efficient and businesslike way

Acknowledgements

The authors are grateful to the following secretaries for their valuable contributions to the case studies:

Susan Amey	Sheila Harris
Lyn Applin	Sylvia Hennen
Marion Bateman	Janette Horswell
Jeanne Brown	Kim Hunt
Hazel Churcher	Karen Irving
Vivienne Coleshill	Jill Lindemere
Maggie Cotter	Nicola Lord
Joan Cuthbert	Kate Lovegrove
Brenda Discombe	Vera Mould
Marina Doglio	Nicola Parry
Anne Douglas	Maureen Queen
Margaret Garden	Dee Saker
Wendy Gardiner	Beryl Smith
Alison Hamlin	Susan Watson

We are also grateful to the London Chamber of Commerce Examinations Board for permission to reproduce and adapt questions from past examination papers and to Judith Stanyer and Simon Cope for material supplied. Our particular thanks go to Bob Mitchell for his help and advice.

ML/JH

Carter, Parker & Watts chartered accountants

HISTORICAL BACKGROUND

Carter & Company (known throughout the UK as Carters) was founded in the year 1860 at 121 Colmore Row in the city of Birmingham by John Selwyn Carter. In the early years of his accountancy career John Carter lived over his office and devoted long hours to his firm, laying sound foundations for its rapid expansion. It was, of course, in the setting of the Industrial Revolution – a favourable one for the practice of accountancy – that John Carter developed his firm, catering especially for the needs of merchants dealing in jewellery and silverware. After 40 years as senior partner, John Carter retired in 1900 and was succeeded by his son, Norman Carter. Norman opened a London office in 1912, and brought in James Parker, as a partner, to take charge of the Birmingham office. Further offices were opened during the first half of the 20th century and in 1960 Carter & Company was amalgamated with RA Watts & Co to establish an even larger national network of accountancy offices, represented in over 20 towns and cities throughout the country.

CASE STUDY ORGANISATION

This case study relates to the Oxford office of Carter, Parker & Watts, formed in 1970 by merger with a small partnership, Watkins & Parkinson. With the backing of the national reputation of Carters, the office grew rapidly to its present size with seven partners and a total staff of 110, including 15 secretarial staff.

The partners

Each partner has responsibility for an area of work, as well as looking after the interests of a number of clients. The organisation chart on page 4 shows how the responsibilities are divided between the partners. Carters attaches a great deal of importance to providing clients with the best possible service and this is always a major consideration when changes in organisation are contemplated. The firm also takes every opportunity to be involved in the local community. Mr Priest, the partner in charge, is a magistrate and a governor of the local college of technology. Another partner, Graham Summers, represents the firm at chamber of commerce meetings and other members of staff are encouraged to belong to local organisations and participate in their events.

The partners hold a partnership meeting in the boardroom at 1000 hrs on the first Tuesday of every month, the partner in charge taking the chair for these meetings. All partners are expected to attend to discuss the overall progress and policies of the firm. Full staff meetings are held periodically, although with the increased numbers of staff this is becoming extremely difficult.

Recent changes in the organisation of the firm include the appointment of a specialist personnel manager as well as the setting up of a secretarial support group.

Personnel administration

Mrs Angela Barnes's appointment as personnel manager was long overdue to assist Mr Morley in staffing matters. Mrs Barnes was also asked to be responsible for health and safety matters and to give them priority in her initial programme of work.

Secretarial services

A change in the organisation of secretarial assistance resulted from concern shown by both partners and staff over the amount of overtime worked, together with the increasing use made of word processors. All clients' accounts are now computerised and kept on disc, reducing the amount of typing and checking, as the current year's entries are automatically recalled from memory to become the previous year's entries in the succeeding year. See the specimen balance sheet on page 5.

The majority of typewritten work in this firm is concerned with clients' accounts and reports and, in view of the increased use of computers for such work, it was centralised into a newly-formed section called the Secretarial Support Group (SSG). One of the senior secretaries, Miss Rosemary Cobb, was given the task of supervising the work of the section. One of her first tasks was to call a special meeting of the section to explain how the SSG would operate and attempt to allay any fears concerning the new system and her involvement in it. As a result of this change, the partners' secretaries were relieved of the task of preparing clients' accounts and were able to concentrate fully on the personal needs of the partners. However, Mrs Perkins, as senior secretary, assumed overall responsibility for the Secretarial Support Group.

Most of the dictation and instructions received in the SSG are recorded on dictation machines or handwritten and, as a result of the centralisation, the workflow can be controlled more efficiently than previously when typists were allocated to different departments. All typists are called secretaries, but

Mrs Perkins admits that this is misleading as most are employed for much of their time as word processing operators and do not undertake the full range of secretarial duties.

Mrs Perkins has been with the firm for nine years, working for the partner in charge for the last five years. Mr Priest became partner in charge six months ago following the death of Mr Charles Broad, the previous head of the firm. Mr Priest was appointed from outside the firm, but knew the locality well from a previous appointment held in the city. Mrs Perkins is now familiar with her new employer's methods of working, although at first she found it difficult to adjust. She particularly likes the way he involves her in organising the 'public relations' events such as the post-budget seminars held at local hotels and the firm's involvement in the local community, which includes entertaining guests at the varsity cricket match.

Secretaries are responsible for filing the partners' correspondence, but all other filing is centralised and carried out by the filing clerks. Copiers are installed on every floor of the office block and staff do their own copying of small quantities. Larger quantities are reproduced by the staff in the office management section. Telex and fax transmission facilities are operated by the receptionists, although it is possible for partners' secretaries to transmit telex messages direct from their word processors.

Staff appraisal schemes are in operation for the accountancy professional staff but not for secretarial staff. Mr Priest is aware that appraisal of secretarial staff should be introduced and has suggested that Mrs Perkins and Mrs Barnes might now begin discussions on methods of introducing such a scheme.

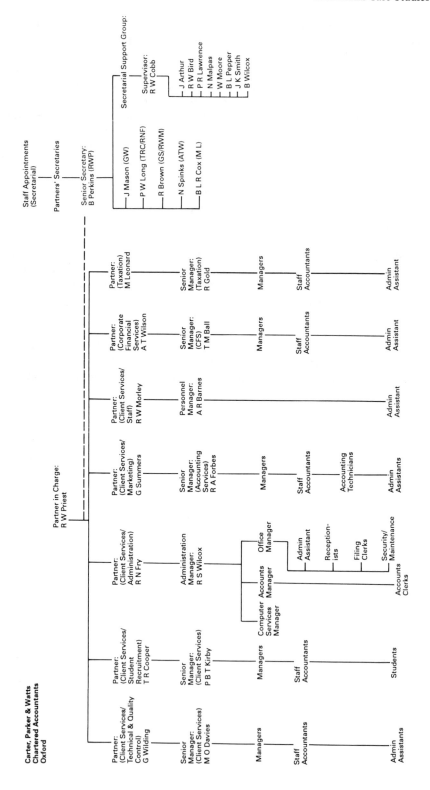

Carter, Parker & Watts
Chartered Accountants
Oxford

Partner in Charge:
R W Priest

Staff Appointments
(Secretarial)

Partners' Secretaries

Senior Secretary:
B Perkins (RWP)

J Mason (GW)

P W Long (TRC/RNF)

R Brown (GS/RWM)

N Spinks (ATW)

B L R Cox (M L)

Secretarial Support Group:

Supervisor:
R W Cobb

J Arthur
R W Bird
P R Lawrence
N Malpas
W Moore
B L Pepper
J K Smith
B Wilcox

Partner:
(Client Services/
Technical & Quality
Control)
G Wilding

Partner:
(Client Services/
Student
Recruitment)
T R Cooper

Partner:
(Client Services/
Administration)
R N Fry

Partner:
(Client Services/
Marketing)
G Summers

Partner:
(Client Services/
Staff)
R W Morley

Partner:
(Corporate
Financial
Services)
A T Wilson

Partner:
(Taxation)
M Leonard

Senior
Manager:
(Client Services)
M O Davies

Senior
Manager:
(Client Services)
P B T Kirby

Administration
Manager:
R S Wilcox

Senior
Manager:
(Accounting
Services)
R A Forbes

Personnel
Manager:
A R Barnes

Senior
Manager:
(CFS)
T M Ball

Senior
Manager:
(Taxation)
R Gold

Managers

Staff
Accountants

Managers

Staff
Accountants

Computer
Services
Manager

Accounts
Manager

Office
Manager

Admin
Assistant

Reception-
ists

Filing
Clerks

Security/
Maintenance

Accounts
Clerks

Managers

Staff
Accountants

Accounting
Technicians

Admin
Assistants

Admin
Assistant

Managers

Staff
Accountants

Admin
Assistant

Managers

Staff
Accountants

Admin
Assistant

Admin
Assistants

Students

Classic Reproductions Limited

Balance Sheet at 31 December 19–2

	19–2	19–1
	£	£
Fixed assets		
Tangible fixed assets	623 405	607 731
Investments	143 359	126 743
	766 764	734 474
Current assets		
Stocks	19 426	28 169
Debtors	30 628	22 128
Bank and cash balance	81 319	82 544
	131 373	132 841
Current liabilities		
Creditors due within one year	(92 416)	(110 455)
Net current assets	38 957	22 386
Total assets *less* current liabilities	805 721	756 860
Provisions for liabilities and charges	(89 035)	(75 735)
Net assets	£716 686	£681 125
Capital and reserves		
Called-up share capital	550 000	550 000
Revaluation reserve	77 000	64 000
Profit and loss account	89 686	67 125
	£716 686	£681 125

The financial statements were approved by the Board
of Directors on 31 January 19–– and were signed on
its behalf by   )
)
)
)
)

WHAT DO YOU THINK?

SECRETARIAL PROCEDURES

1.1 What are the advantages of centralising the typing and word processing services at Carters?

1.2 What factors would you consider when deciding whether to send documents by mail, telex or fax?

1.3 Mrs Barnes has been asked to give health and safety top priority – as a starting point advise her what the employer's obligations are under the Health and Safety at Work Act 1974 and whether the employees have any obligations under this Act.

1.4 If you were responsible for arranging the partners' monthly meetings, what would you expect to do, assuming that you attended the meetings to record the minutes?

STRUCTURE OF BUSINESS

1.5 As it is difficult to accommodate everyone for full staff meetings, what alternative methods of communication could Carters use?

1.6 Discuss the differences between line and staff relationships in the organisation chart. Do any of the staff at Carters have a functional relationship?

1.7 Why does this firm operate as a partnership? How does this type of business unit differ from a sole trader?

1.8 What is a balance sheet and what help is it to management? Comment on the net profit realised in relation to capital employed for both years.

SECRETARIAL ADMINISTRATION

1.9 What 'staffing matters' will Mrs Barnes take over from Mr Morley? If Mrs Barnes computerises the personnel records, are there any legal requirements involved? If so, explain what they are. What information would you expect her to record?

1.10 Why do you think Carters calls all its typists 'secretaries'? What other duties would you expect secretaries to perform?

1.11 How would you expect Mrs Perkins to respond to a change of employer, following the death of Mr Charles Broad? In what ways can his secretary be of assistance to him in settling in to his new position?

1.12 Why do you think Carters attaches so much importance to 'public relations'? In what other ways might good PR be fostered at Carters?

MANAGEMENT APPRECIATION

1.13 How would you advise Miss Cobb to overcome the initial resistance by the typists to her role as their supervisor?

1.14 Apart from involvement in the local community, what other advantages could be gained from Mr Summers' involvement with the local chamber of commerce?

1.15 Why do you think Mr Priest wishes to have a staff appraisal scheme for secretaries? Who do you think should be responsible for conducting such a scheme and why? What questions should be asked at a staff appraisal interview? Devise a suitable form for this purpose.

1.16 How far should Mrs Perkins delegate work to Miss Cobb for the secretarial support group? How could she monitor her performance? What limitations would there be?

ADDITIONAL STUDENT LEARNING ACTIVITIES

FIND OUT

What major changes were announced in the last budget and how they would affect Carters.

ROLE PLAY

Rosemary Cobb's meeting with the secretaries in the SSG – to explain how the newly-formed section will operate and their changed relationships.

Television Vectis

GENERAL BACKGROUND

This case study is about a company we have called Television Vectis for case study purposes, which employs approximately 600 staff at their Television Centre in Southam City. The organisation chart on page 11 indicates the departmental structure of the company.

Independent Television is made up of 15 totally separate companies, each under different ownership, but working together to produce a co-ordinated output of programmes for ITV throughout the UK. Each company is responsible for a particular geographical area, eg Television Vectis covers Southampshire, Ruddleshire and County Gale. The London area has two companies, Isis Television, which is responsible for weekday viewing, and City Weekend Television, which takes over from Friday night to Sunday night. The television companies vary considerably in size, from Isis Television which employs about 2250 staff to Island Television which employs about 70 staff.

The main function of the companies is to make programmes and many of the programmes are put into a central pool for showing throughout the network. The essence of Independent Television is that as far as possible it should provide a regional service and all companies are therefore expected to produce programmes of a local nature for local viewing in addition to their network commitments. These are usually news and magazine programmes.

Independent Television is very different from most other businesses. The products of the business are, of course, the programmes, but these do not provide the main source of income. Some programmes may be sold abroad, but in the main market – the UK – programmes are shown free to the customers. The income to make the programmes and to pay all other costs is mainly produced by the sales staff who sell advertising time at prices determined by programme audience ratings.

The co-ordinating body for the television companies is the Independent Television Companies Association (ITCA). The Network Planning Committee of ITCA consists mainly of representatives of the companies, and meets regularly to plan the advance network schedules.

The Independent Broadcasting Authority (IBA) is the controlling body for

Independent Television. Senior members of the IBA are appointed by the Home Office. The main functions of the IBA are:

1 To select programme companies
2 To supervise programme planning
3 To control advertising
4 To transmit programmes

THE TRAINING FUNCTION

Sally Ann, the Training Co-ordinator, occupies a 'key' position in the training and development of staff potential and especially with the secretaries employed at the Television Centre, as will be seen in the following extracts from her job description:

- Carries out initial evaluation of all training requisitions in consultation with management at all levels
- Carries out careers counselling
- Liaises with managing agents with regard to the supervision of YTS trainees
- Works directly with the Training Manager on management problem solving techniques
- Designs and mounts in-company office skills training courses, eg short-hand and typewriting; telephone technique; minute-taking; interview technique, etc
- Sits on Safety Committee as Training Management Representative
- Takes delegated executive responsibility to set up in-house and external First Aid Training Courses
- Has delegated executive authority to supervise the activities of the Training Department secretary and assignment of work
- Maintains the TVV library of journals, books, teaching videos and presentation skills equipment
- Keeps records of all training activities
- Has delegated executive responsibility to approve, place and oversee all work experience students
- Undertakes the duties and responsibilities of the TVV Pre-retirement Counsellor introducing staff to the pre-retirement programme

The Training Co-ordinator's main role is to plan, supervise and assess the in-house training courses and to arrange for staff to attend external courses. Sally Ann sometimes has difficulty in convincing staff and their superiors of the importance of regular training for staff development. The pressures of the job often impinge on attendance at courses and it creates problems when staff withdraw from courses at short notice. The external courses usually have to be booked a month or so in advance and Sally Ann has to remind staff, otherwise they are inclined to forget them.

A total of 2306 days of training were organised last year made up as follows:

Engineering	405
Site services	120
Personnel	248
Production	486
Administration	185
Programmes	473
Finance	389

The Training Co-ordinator organises inter-departmental meetings on training matters to provide a forum for the discussion of training needs and to communicate new developments in the provision of training. Her training records are currently kept on index cards but she is considering methods of computerising them. Sally Ann also spends a considerable amount of time dealing with the many school leavers who apply to TVV for work experience and she conducts short induction courses for them.

OFFICE SERVICES

Most office services, such as the postroom, reprographics, reception, tele-communications and stationery supplies, are centralised at TVV under the control of the Administration Manager. Travel arrangements are undertaken by secretaries using the services of local travel agents, but the use of company cars is controlled by the Administration Manager. Each department keeps its own files under the supervision and control of the secretaries.

Specialist secretarial positions at TVV

The secretarial positions of special interest in a TV company are those concerned with the production of programmes, ie programme secretary and production secretary.

A programme secretary, who needs to be a fast, accurate typist with a good telephone manner, has to deal with the following:

- answer viewers' queries
- type verbatim scripts from videos
- arrange for despatch riders to deliver scripts to various parts of the country
- organise exhibitions
- type facts sheets
- type and issue releases of future programmes
- maintain contact with public libraries for research into programmes

The production secretary is in charge of the office when the rest of the production team is out on location and he or she has to use initiative when dealing with enquiries. The secretary has to work under considerable pressure and often at unsocial hours. The job includes:

- typing draft scripts (*see* example on page 12)
- drawing up and typing schedules

- typing camera cards
- organising and administering actors' hotel bookings, expenses, fees, etc

Staff appraisal

Staff appraisal awareness courses are organised annually by the Personnel Manager to enable staff to measure their performance against agreed targets.

Staff relations

A monthly magazine for all the staff of Television Vectis provides information about new programmes, staff changes and social activities. A Sports and Social Club organises social activities for the staff including dances, outings, hockey, golf, yachting and angling.

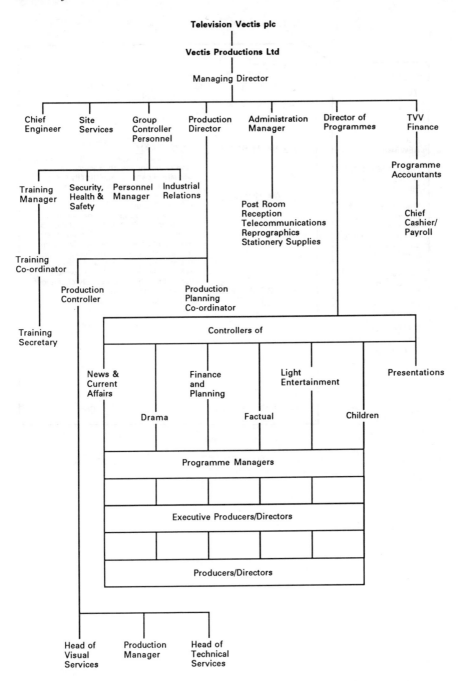

Television Vectis plc

Vectis Productions Ltd

Managing Director

Chief Engineer	Site Services	Group Controller Personnel	Production Director	Administration Manager	Director of Programmes	TVV Finance

Programme Accountants

Training Manager	Security, Health & Safety	Personnel Manager	Industrial Relations

Post Room
Reception
Telecommunications
Reprographics
Stationery Supplies

Chief Cashier/ Payroll

Training Co-ordinator

Production Controller

Production Planning Co-ordinator

Training Secretary

Controllers of

News & Current Affairs		Finance and Planning		Light Entertainment		Presentations

Drama

Factual

Children

Programme Managers

Executive Producers/Directors

Producers/Directors

Head of Visual Services	Production Manager	Head of Technical Services

NOTE: Secretaries are employed by all senior executives, production teams and programme teams.

A Television Script

MONDAY

ITV

TVV

6.00 pm
NEWSNET

FRED FEARLESS
FIONA FULSOME
MIKE DRIVELL

The latest news &
pictures with Fred
Fearless & Fiona
Fulsome in the City
and Mike Drivell
in the County.

Editors:
Joe Cuttem
Mark Space
Exec. Producer
Ivor Rule

TVV Production

TVV Times

NEWSNET	Item 7 (1)
Mon 14-Dec-19-- 15:55:43	LINK TO RUDDLETON SCHOOL
GUS MENDEL	

1. CAM   FRED   FRED TO CAM./
                     Later in the programme . . . the top dogs
                     who're tucking into their very own
                     Christmas party . . . and the city centre
                     that's laying on a high wire act to
2. CAM   FIONA   attract the shoppers./
                     FIONA TO CAM.
                     But first . . . youngsters from a primary
                     school in Ruddleshire have just picked
                     up an award . . . for transforming their
                     garden into a haven for wildlife. When
                     the school was built fifteen years ago,
                     the plot was just wasteland. Now, with
                     only a little help from the grown-ups
                     the children have completely changed it
3. ENG RUDDLETON   Sally Stunner reports./
     SCHOOL   FULL ENG.

/IN:

(CAP GEN TBA)   Cont....

THE QUESTIONS ARE . . .

SECRETARIAL PROCEDURES

2.1 What method could Sally Ann use to remind staff about their training commitments?

2.2 Draw up a checklist for organising a training conference at TVV to deal with the major provisions of the Data Protection Act 1984. What are the major provisions of this Act?

2.3 TVV staff received a total of 2306 days training last year. The Training Manager has asked you to supply this information visually indicating the number of training hours completed by each department. Illustrate the type of chart you would recommend for this purpose.

2.4 In what ways do you consider the production secretary would have to use initiative when the production team was out on location?

STRUCTURE OF BUSINESS

2.5 (*a*) How does the financing of an ITV company differ from that of the BBC?
(*b*) Discuss the effects on TVV of the proposed changes in the operation of television in the UK.

2.6 What role has the Finance Department at Vectis Productions Ltd? What is its relationship with the other departments?

2.7 The sale of television programmes abroad provides a portion of the income for TVV. What is the significance of this for the UK balance of payments?

2.8 What are the purposes of an organisation chart? Would any of the staff at TVV have a staff/line relationship?

SECRETARIAL ADMINISTRATION

2.9 What major items should Sally Ann include in an in-company training course on minute-taking? How would you arrange for the participants to receive some practical experience in recording minutes?

2.10 Suggest how the Training Co-ordinator should try to overcome the problems created by staff withdrawing from courses at short notice.

2.11 What steps should be taken to computerise training records? What information should be recorded and how would the Training Section benefit from a computerised system?

2.12 A programme secretary needs to be a fast, accurate typist with a good telephone manner. What other qualities and skills would you expect in applicants for this post? How would you advise the programme secretary in dealing with press enquiries?

MANAGEMENT APPRECIATION

2.13 How would you suggest Sally Ann should overcome the difficulty of convincing staff and their superiors of the importance of regular training for staff development?

2.14 What is 'delegated executive authority' in relation to Sally Ann's job at TVV?

2.15 The Training Co-ordinator works directly with the Training Manager on management problem-solving techniques. Explain two of these techniques which might be used at TVV.

2.16 Why do you think TVV organises staff appraisal courses with groups of staff? Is this method better than holding interviews with individuals? As such courses are considered important, what management aspects do you think such appraisals aim to satisfy?

ADDITIONAL STUDENT LEARNING ACTIVITIES

FIND OUT

What journals, books, teaching videos and presentation skills equipment should be kept in the TVV library for the training of secretaries.

ROLE PLAY

Sally Ann's introductory talk at the induction course for work experience students.
Other members of the group can role play the training secretary, the programme secretary and the production secretary explaining their jobs to the students.

Pitman Publishing

The subject for this case study is the publisher of this book – Pitman Publishing – and the part played by Nicola Lord who is secretary for the Secretarial Studies and Business Education Division of the Editorial Department. The process of publishing a book is similar in many ways to the manufacturing of any other product, involving the departments you would normally expect to see, such as Accountancy, Production, Sales and Marketing, Personnel and Administration (*see* the organisation chart on page 18). Nicola works in a division of the Editorial Department, one not normally found in a manufacturing concern but which can be equated with research, development and purchasing. For example, the publishers and commissioning editors are engaged in researching proposals for new books; developing ideas with authors to cater for the needs of schools and colleges, taking into account the Government's education and training initiatives; and 'purchasing' the services of authors to write books by issuing contracts.

HISTORICAL BACKGROUND

Pitman first began publishing in 1837 when Sir Isaac Pitman invented his world-famous shorthand system and offered tuition in the art of writing by sound from his 'penny plate'. The first company, Sir Isaac Pitman & Sons, was formed in 1886 to publish shorthand books and by the turn of the century Pitman books were being published on a wide range of commercial and vocational subjects. Following the death of Sir Isaac Pitman in 1897, members of his family assumed responsibility for the firm and developed its activities until 1985 when it was acquired by the Longman Group UK Ltd, extending the range of books it offered to include M & E, Polytech and Longman. The Managing Director, Ian Pringle, in an article for the magazine *Business Education Today* on the occasion of the 150th anniversary of the founding of Pitman Publishing said: 'Over the decades, the name Pitman has become synonymous with, first shorthand, and later the broad area of business education from vocational to professional studies and information technology . . . we are today the leading international publisher of the titles in these important growth areas.' Teachers, students and educationalists were invited to two major events during the anniversary year – a national one-day conference on the theme 'People, Industry and Education' held at Bath and a Royal Society of Arts Fellowship Lecture at which the distinguished historian Lord Asa Briggs reviewed the work of Sir Isaac Pitman, its influence on employment trends in office work and its significant role in Britain's vocational education system.

COMPANY ORGANISATION AND SERVICES

106 staff are employed by Pitman Publishing, 35 of whom are based at the Distribution Centre in Southport where the books are stored and despatched. Some staff belong to trade unions such as NUJ and SOGAT but generally the individual needs of staff are dealt with by managers or at departmental staff meetings. The company employs sales representatives for different regions of the UK and has agents and stockists in Australia, Bangladesh, Botswana, Cameroon, Canada, Caribbean, Ghana, Hong Kong, India, Italy, Japan, Jordan, Kenya, Latin America, Lesotho, Middle East, New Zealand, Nigeria, Pakistan, South Africa, South East Asia, Spain, Swaziland, USA and Zimbabwe.

The sales representatives, indeed all staff at Pitman, are kept informed of developments in the publishing programme of the company by the *repfile*, a type of house journal which is issued monthly. It contains changes in examinations and professional body regulations; student statistics; details of new books and new editions; foreign rights deals; book review quotes; staff changes, etc.

Control of stationery, telecommunications, reception, mailing, safety, security, training and recruitment, selection and employment of staff are all centralised and administered in the Personnel and Administration Department. Filing is administered within each department and in the Editorial Department files are classified by book title or author. Out-of-date files are stored at the Distribution Centre in Southport.

SECRETARIAL STUDIES AND BUSINESS STUDIES DIVISION

Each division of the editorial department employs a secretary who is responsible for the secretarial support services of the division. Nicola Lord is responsible for the secretarial work of the Secretarial Studies and Business Studies Division. She reports to Mr K Roberts, the Manager, and works for a total of six people who require secretarial services in the division. This can create difficulties in determining priorities, but Nicola decides her own work priorities and does it as fairly as she can, accepting that seniority should not necessarily influence her order of work. For example, there are occasions when the Manager's work is not as urgent as the tasks given to her by the

Production Editor. The conflicting demands made on Nicola's time were highlighted on 21 March when the morning began:

- A Production Editor had left some copy typing on her desk containing a letter to an author with some queries on a manuscript which was being copy-edited; a letter to an author enclosing proofs and asking for them to be returned within one week; and a letter commissioning artwork for a book
- The Commissioning Editor called in to ask her to type a long, complicated proposal for a publishing meeting in two days' time. When typed, all six pages had to be photocopied and circulated to six committee members two clear days before the meeting
- An author telephoned requesting an appointment with the Publisher early the following week
- At this point another Publisher's secretary approached her in an agitated state as she had a problem with the word processor and required her help
- On top of all this, the Manager appeared and said he was getting a little behind with his correspondence and could Nicola come in and take some dictation!

Secretary's job description

Nicola's job description includes the following duties:

- providing secretarial support services
- maintaining and initiating departmental records using the in-house computer system
- recording the progress of new projects and new editions and initiating action when requested (see below)
- answering telephone enquiries and dealing with authors in the absence of departmental staff
- using her own judgement in processing routine matters and answering routine correspondence
- liaising with other departments to co-ordinate routine procedures

Editorial office procedure

The steps involved in monitoring the progress of new books and new editions are as follows:

1 Receipt of proposal from author acknowledged.
2 Proposal sent to reviewers as directed by the Publisher.
3 Proposal typed for project meeting.
4 Contract typed and sent to author.
5 Date for completion of manuscript noted.
6 Date for completion of artwork/design of cover noted.
7 Date when manuscript sent to printer noted.
8 Dates noted when proofs are received for checking and when they are returned to the printer.

9 Advance copies of the book received from the printer.

10 Publication date noted.

Nicola uses an electronic typewriter for most of her typing tasks but has shared use with three other secretaries of a word processing facility which has to be booked in advance and, unfortunately, is not always available when required. Nicola is competent in using the word processor and occasionally helps with the training of new staff. She also has access to telex, fax and a copier.

The Publishers are required to supply the Sales and Marketing Department with details of new books and new editions for the catalogues which are published twice yearly. A page from a recent catalogue is given on page 19. The Production Editors control the work involved in checking the proofs when they are received from the printer. It is important that corrections are made clearly so that the printers are in no doubt as to the amendments to be made. An example of a corrected printer's proof is given on page 20.

Nicola organises occasional staff meetings and prepares papers for the project and editorial board meetings. New proposals for books are considered at the twice monthly project meetings which consist of the Managing Director (chairman) and representatives from the marketing, production and editorial departments. Editorial policy matters are discussed at the editorial board meetings comprising the Managing Director, the International Marketing Director and the Publishers from all departments.

Nicola serves as the communication point for the division. She receives the telephone calls for the Manager, Publisher and Editors when they are not available in their offices. She frequently deals with sales and product queries and likes to be given responsibility for organising projects. These may entail organising a conference or lecture (such as the RSA Fellowship Lecture referred to earlier), the launch of a new product, contacting reviewers for new book proposals, etc. A budget of £2500 was allocated for the RSA Fellowship Lecture and Nicola was required to select appropriately priced refreshments and flowers from the quotations received (*see* pages 21 and 22). A further £60 for the cost of printing 250 invitation cards also had to be included in the budget allocation. It was estimated that 175 people would attend this function.

Nicola believes that the manner in which she receives visitors and speaks to people on the telephone is of the utmost importance in establishing good public relations. She has to be discreet and not discuss matters which are the responsibility of others, eg a point concerning the editing of a book.

Pitman Publishing

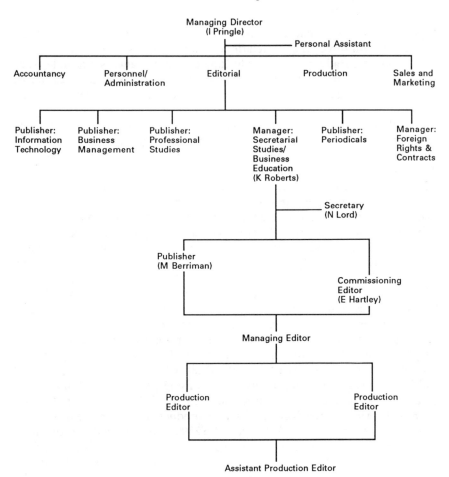

Pitman New Era Shorthand
Anniversary Edition
Facility Drills
Julie Watson

An ideal aid for the students, this book provides the extra practice needed when learning shorthand.

May 1988 / 96 pp / Paper / £3.95
ISBN 0 273 02904 5

NEW EDITION

Secretarial Duties
8th edition
John Harrison

Secretarial Duties is a classic text that is known throughout the world for its comprehensive coverage of the subject. This eighth edition includes a greater number and range of in-tray exercises to enable the student to develop problem-solving skills as well as to apply the student's theoretical knowledge to practical and realistic work situations.

- *includes new chapters on mailing procedures and equipment, pay and contracts of employment, and information technology*
- *fully meets the requirements of the RSA, BTEC National, LCC and PEI examinations in Secretarial Duties and office profile*
- *plenty of in-tray exercises and assignments for class work*

April 1988 352 pages Paper
ISBN 0 273 02665 8 £6.95

Locoscript
Anne Clark and Kath Butler

Written specifically for Locoscript for use on the Amstrad, this book is a useful addition to the very successful range of existing Word Processor Training Guides. These guides are exceptionally comprehensive and easy-to-use and ideal for anyone wishing to acquire word processing skills quickly.

June 1988 64 pages Paper
ISBN 0 273 02916 9 £3.50

326   Secretarial Duties

- Filing and indexing her employer's personal and business correspondence.   Ψ

- Organising and attending meetings, including the preparation of agenda and minutes.

- Organising her employer's office, ie keeping his Wall-charts up to date and controlling his papers and files.   ⌣

- Generally relieving the employer of many of his routine business and private matters.

- Supplying information, ie using teletext services and knowing the books and other sources where it can be found.

- Taking care of her employer's petty cash and bank transaction.   s/ o

- Supervision of junior secretarial staff.

- Complying with the requirements of the health and safety at work Act, 1974.   ≡/

- Establishing procedures and practices to ensure confidentiality and security of information.

- Controlling stationery and office materials for her employer's and her own use. Organising conferences and social activities.

The secretary's day

The secretary's day seldom follows a set pattern and no two secretarial posts are alike, but the following list of activities is representative of a typical day in the life of a secretary:

At the beginning of the day:

- Collect the employers mail from the mail room date stamp it and attach it to the relevant files.   open and

- Refer to your diary to ascertain your employer's and your own engagements for the day locate relevant files and papers in connection with these and bring forward any files requiring action.

- Place all incoming mails and files (brought forward) in your employer's 'in tray'.

- Draw attention of your employer to any items urgent in the or the day's activities.   mail

- Check that the entries in your diary correspond with those in your employer's diary.

Printers' proof for a new edition of
Secretarial Duties

COPES
CUISINE

99-103 Lomond Grove, LONDON SE5 7HN.   Tel: 01 701 1960/01 708 0628

13 May 19–

Our ref: SGC/PRK

Miss Nicola Lord
Pitman Publishing
128 Long Acre
London WC2E 9AN

Dear Miss Lord

Further to our meeting last Friday, I would like to give you an estimate
for your catering requirements on 23 September 19– for 175 people.

I would like to suggest the following cocktail menu:

Cocktail Food @ £5.00 per head + VAT

>   Scotch smoked salmon triangles
>   Assorted dips with various crudities and corn chips
>   Strawberries and mozzarella on sticks
>   Cocktail sausages glazed with honey and ginger
>   Wantons served with apricot sauce
>   Oriental chicken tartlets
>   Roquefort grapes
>   Salami cornets
>   Devilled prawns
>   Deep fried mushrooms served with Stilton mayonnaise

> Alternatively, the
> price for this menu
> excluding strawberries
> and mozzarella on
> sticks and salami
> cornets would be £4.45
> per head + VAT.

Wines and Soft Drinks

As discussed we shall provide the following wines and soft drinks on a
sale or return basis:

Muscadet	@ £4.75 per bottle
Cote du Rhone	@ £4.25 per bottle
Orange juice	@ £1.20 per litre
Tomato juice	@ £0.45 per bottle
Perrier	@ £1.00 per litre
Coca cola	@ £0.45 per can

I suggest that we allow a budget of £3.25 per head.

Hired Equipment

We shall provide the following:

>   Ashtrays, sherry trays, 6' x 9' cloths, 8 medium blue and gold cloths,
>   blue service cloths for the price (including delivery) of £92.60 + VAT.

>   Naturally, all ice, glasses and water jugs will be provided at no extra
>   charge as we are providing all wines and soft drinks.

Waiting Staff

Assuming 175 guests are expected, I would like to suggest 2 waiters and
6 waitresses and if you pay them direct the fee would be £188.00 in total.

Finally, I believe your guests are expected at 6.00 pm so our staff will
arrive at 5.00 pm.

I shall look forward to receiving your instructions in the very near
future.

Yours sincerely

Simon G Cope

Judith Stanyer

Florist

493 Kingston Road, London SW20 8JP.
Telephone: 01-540 1663

12 May 19–

Miss Nicola Lord
Pitman Publishing
128 Long Acre
London WC2E 9AN

Dear Miss Lord

In reply to your letter of 8 May, we shall be pleased to supply you with flowers for the Evening Lecture to be held at the Royal Society of Arts in London. Our prices for the various arrangements that could be used for the refreshment tables are as follows:

	Price each £
Posy arrangements	5.00
Long low/oval arrangements	15.00
Buffet table front facing arrangements	20.00
All round buffet arrangement	25.00
Pedestal arrangement or front facing table arrangement	40.00
Vases of flowers loosely arranged	5.00

We hope that you will find these prices satisfactory and we will look forward to hearing from you in the future.

Yours sincerely

Judith Stanyer

Judith Stanyer
Florist

VAT Reg. No.: 451 1517 79

WHAT ARE YOUR VIEWS?

SECRETARIAL PROCEDURES

3.1 What factors would you take into consideration when deciding which files should be removed from the cabinet and despatched to the Distribution Centre? How could you gain access to the contents of files once they have been removed?

3.2 Illustrate a visual planning chart which Nicola could use to monitor progress of new projects and new editions.

3.3 Say how you would organise a system for sharing the use of the word processor between the four users. Is there a case for each secretary to be allocated a word processor? Give your reasons 'for' or 'against'.

3.4 Mr Roberts frequently travels by car to schools and colleges throughout the UK to discuss new proposals for books with teachers and authors. What arrangements would Nicola be expected to make for him prior to his departure and during his absence?

STRUCTURE OF BUSINESS

3.5 What is the importance of research, design and development for a publisher such as Pitman?

3.6 Select two departments of Pitman Publishing and explain their inter-relationship.

3.7 Publishers take account of the Government's education and training initiatives when researching proposals for new books. Outline the Government's current role in encouraging training for work.

3.8 Which staff at Pitman do you consider might be members of NUJ and SOGAT? What is the role of the unions in industrial relations?

SECRETARIAL ADMINISTRATION

3.9 Draw up a checklist of the action required by Nicola to organise the RSA Fellowship Lecture, indicating when action would be initiated. Say what you would do:
(*a*) before the day of the lecture;
(*b*) on the day of the lecture; and
(*c*) during the following week.
Include your recommendations for refreshments and floral decorations for the refreshment tables, with regard to the budget allocated for this function.

3.10 What is the difference between public relations and advertising? In what ways can Nicola enhance her company's public relations?

3.11 If you were in Nicola's position how would you have prioritised her work on the morning of 21 March and what, if anything, would you have said to the protagonists?

3.12 Why do you think Nicola sees herself as the 'communication point' for her division? What methods of communication might she use for urgent communications with (*a*) the distribution centre; (*b*) sales representatives; and (*c*) overseas agents?

MANAGEMENT APPRECIATION

3.13 Suggest a recruitment and selection procedure which could be adopted by the Personnel and Administration Department.

3.14 What are the advantages and disadvantages of centralising the office services within the Personnel and Administration Department?

3.15 'A major contribution that computers have made to management is the provision of a wider range of information, more quickly and accurately than was previously available.' (LCC Private and Executive Secretary's Diploma). Select 3 of the departments at Pitman and explain by examples the kind of management activity which can be computer-aided.

3.16 The publisher of management books is examining a proposal for a book on management appreciation. The first chapter purports to explain the contribution to management knowledge of some well-known management theorists. Suggest three such theorists which you would expect the author to include and say what contributions each made.

ADDITIONAL STUDENT LEARNING ACTIVITIES

FIND OUT

on a map of the world where Pitman has
agents
OR
rules for typing authors' manuscripts
and
the commonly-used printers' correction signs

ROLE PLAY

Nicola's introduction to word processing
when training a new secretary at Pitman –
say what the word processor will do and how
it is used at Pitman.

Esso UK plc

GENERAL BACKGROUND

The company was first established in the United Kingdom in 1888 under the name of the Anglo-American Oil Company. Today, the company's organisation consists of a holding company, Esso UK plc, with two operating companies:

1 Esso Exploration and Production UK Ltd responsible for the exploration and production of crude oil and natural gas;
2 Esso Petroleum Co Ltd responsible for the refining, distribution and marketing of petroleum products throughout the UK.

Exxon Corporation in the USA is the ultimate shareholder of the Esso UK plc group of companies (*see* the organisation chart on page 29). Exxon is considered to be one of the world's most profitable companies and has a total workforce of some 100 000, approximately 4500 of these being employed in the UK. Oil supplies one-third of Britain's energy and has vital non-energy uses, such as lubrication and the manufacture of chemicals. Esso provides one-fifth of the petroleum products used in the UK market and is a major producer of offshore oil and gas through its joint operations with Shell in the North Sea. The discovery of offshore oil and gas has transformed Britain's energy position. Since 1981, oil production has exceeded consumption – making the UK a net exporter of crude oil – and close to 80 per cent of total UK gas demand is met by indigenous production. Esso's production of crude oil and natural gas accounts for some 15 per cent of total UK oil and gas output. The company currently has an interest in 14 producing offshore oil and gas fields, with more under active development.

Esso sells directly to over 1200 industrial/commercial customers and indirectly to more than 100 000 who buy Esso products through the company's authorised distributors, including nationalised industries, government departments and public utilities. Computer based systems for handling customers' orders operate at key centres. These centres are consolidated at West London Terminal to form a single Esso Orderpoint serving the whole of the UK. There are also an enormous number of individual customers, using nearly 3000 service stations, a third of which are owned by the company and over 830 Esso shops retail a wide range of goods.

An offshore oil field – one of many associated with the joint operations of Esso and Shell in the North Sea.

Company communications

A fortnightly magazine called *Newsline* is distributed to staff throughout Esso's organisation in the UK to disseminate information concerning new developments and changes in organisation; staff news; retail news; training programmes, safety and security matters; social activities; etc. An article featured in *Newsline* dealing with the computerisation of buying and paying for goods is reproduced on page 31. Modern telephone, telex, fax and electronic mail systems are used throughout the organisation for both internal and external communications.

Safety and security

Strict safety and security measures are in force at Esso both at operating and office locations. For example, in the Production Department offices of Esso Exploration and Production UK Ltd quarterly safety meetings are held for the entire staff and committees involving representatives from every floor of the head office meet on a regular basis. Security is controlled from the reception office and visitors are required to sign in a visitors' book and wear labels when visiting the building.

CASE STUDY SITUATION

This case study features the work of Nicola Parry who is secretary to two senior executives, the Technical Manager and one of the Operations Managers of Esso Exploration and Production UK Ltd. The Technical Manager, Mr Docherty, when asked what he expected from his secretary, said that she must be fully conversant with new technology in the office; adaptable to cope with constant changes in systems; possess impeccable inter-personal skills; be competent in organising meetings, appointments and visitors; and be efficient in office administration, including filing and timely, effective retrieval. He drafts much of his correspondence on the train during his two-hour daily journeys commuting to and from London and although he makes some use of shorthand and audio dictation, this is not extensive.

The secretary, Nicola, who had been promoted from a position as word processing operator, described the tasks in her job as follows:

- Opening and distributing incoming mail
- Typing correspondence – mainly technical reports, memos and presentation material (an extract from a memo is given on page 30). Correspondence to Exxon in America, as well as to Esso locations throughout the UK, is sent by electronic mail
- Making travel arrangements, including itineraries for complex journeys, booking hotels by telex and keeping a record of overseas travel for the department
- Scheduling and organising meetings, which involves agreeing dates with other secretaries; notifying staff of meeting dates; booking the conference room with the receptionist; arranging for visual aids to be available; and ordering refreshments (either contacting a local sandwich bar to provide snacks on the premises, booking into a restaurant, or organising caterers and waitresses on the premises for special functions)
- Completing expenses forms from receipts and vouchers
- Compiling a holiday schedule for the department
- Recording time sheets showing the amount of time the managers spend on each project
- Typing viewgraphs (another name for overhead projector transparencies)

for presentations, with the secretary using her discretion in the layout and presentation of data

- Keeping the diaries for the managers and making appointments. There are occasions when Nicola has to rearrange appointments when the Manager has independently made another conflicting appointment. She uses a card index system for recalling names, addresses and telephone numbers frequently used
- Filing of current correspondence. This is classified by subject. A central filing section stores files no longer regularly required by the department, and acts as an archive for files which are no longer of operational use
- Copying documents on the photocopier
- Using the administrative computing system (ACS) for sending messages to other staff, including dates of meetings. This computerised office system incorporates electronic mail, word processing, diaries and spreadsheets
- Bringing forward matters which require the attention of the executives
- Covering for other senior secretaries in the department when they are absent as it is less appropriate for the senior managers to use temps
- Helping with occasional personal matters for the managers in so far as they interact with the work situation, such as medical appointments, holiday arrangements, etc

Nicola enjoys her work, especially the contacts with the company's executives and with personnel from other companies. She responds well to working under pressure, which is a requirement of the job, and also accepts that there will be occasions when she has to stay late in order to complete an urgent job.

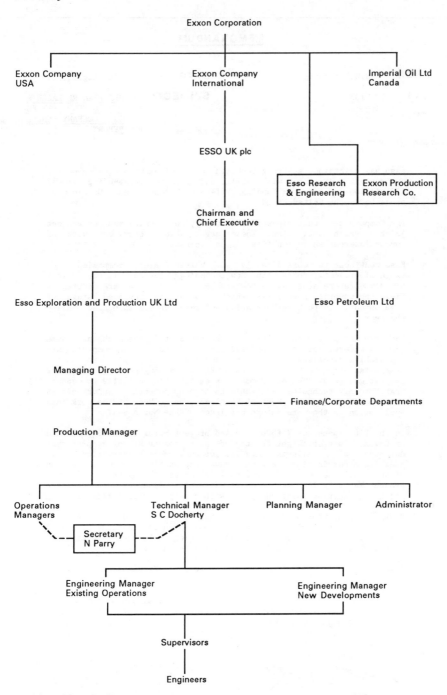

Extract of Organisation Chart

MEMORANDUM

FROM: S.C. Docherty   **DATE:**   16th August, 19--

EXT: 3105   **SUBJECT:** <u>UPSTREAM RESEARCH &
                                              DEVELOPMENT TEXT FOR</u>
TO: File   <u>19-- COMPANY ANNUAL
                                              REPORT</u>

Esso has maintained a strong research and development programme on its
own account and jointly with Shell, and is currently spending around
£20 million a year on funding offshore Research and Development
projects in the United Kingdom.

The Company has participated in industry, university and government
joint research activities. These organisations carry out work of
common interest which benefits all participants.

Esso continues to work directly with United Kingdom companies on a
range of projects to develop new technology for use in the United
Kingdom offshore area and elsewhere in the world. We are currently
financing several programmes which are at an advanced stage of
development. Support for new areas of research was announced during
the year.

The Esso Deepwater Integrated Production System research programme
(EDIPS) entered its fourth phase during 1987 and British companies are
researching diverless maintenance and tension leg platform tether
pre-installation techniques, with FUEL Subsea Engineering acting as
project managers. The programme was established initially to ensure
that Esso has technology available to develop potential opportunities
which may exist in the West of Shetland area. Much of the work has
application in the more mature provinces of the North Sea.

In the final phase of a £500 thousand project Marex Technology Limited
of Cowes, Isle of Wight is conducting a sea trial of a prototype
databuoy which collects detailed oceanographic information. In
addition Marex is field testing a wave compensation system, a version
of which will be built for use on floating rigs. By the end of the
project Marex will have an advanced product line of oceanographic
measuring and processing equipment with high potential for export.

Research into enhanced oil recovery has also continued, with Redwood
Corex (Services) Limited and Robertson Research International Limited
examining miscible drive and polymer-flooding techniques respectively.
This work will be applicable in the North Sea and elsewhere.

Esso continues to contribute both management and technical expertise
to these projects which are aimed at lower cost production techniques
for existing and potential new developments. It is also making a
substantial contribution to enhancing the technical capability of the
United Kingdom offshore supply industry. As a result the British
supply companies involved are better equipped to position themselves
to compete in world markets and also acquire expertise which can be
applied in the United Kingdom North Sea.

S.C. Docherty

GOING LIVE

In December, Secretary's and Administration Department was the first to put the SAP Beeline system, which matches orders and invoices, into use. *Newsline* took stock of the situation

FINDING A SYSTEM that streamlined procedures for buying and paying for goods and services was the task set for Contracts and Materials and Accounts Payable. After exhaustive trials, Beeline was the system duly installed, an impressive package supplied by SAP and used to advantage in over 200 other leading international companies.

C&M and Accounts Payable proved the complex software package a success in Esso, so the next step was to extend its use to other areas of the Company. Secretary's and Administration Department agreed to be top of the list.

Iris Dean, analyst, and business coordinator Brian Cafferkey from Planning and Controls played a key role in implementing the system within S&A. "To meet our year-end deadline we devoted two people from within our own department to the project," said Iris.

August saw the duo begin the process of refining the aspects of the system that most complemented S&A's needs. Said Brian: "We had to review the whole department was involved in purchasing: the level of activity in each division, how much money was being spent and who with."

Brian and Iris went on to develop an eight-stage training module, run in November, to equip the 30-strong team to 'go live' with the system a month later.

Briefly, Beeline works like this: an order for supplies is placed on the system. When the goods are received the order is recalled on-screen and the goods are checked in. Accounts Payable can then enter invoice details allowing S&A to check that the invoice, order and goods received match, and payment can be issued.

Although hard copies of an order *can* be printed out, the paperless system is the ultimate aim. No more problems with illegible handwriting, or missing documents lost in transit from one department to another. All the information required is available at the touch of a button.

As the first 'end-user' department to come to grips with Beeline, what have been the immediate advantages? Explained Iris: "Already we have been able to build up a history of our expenditure and can go on to control the department's budget more accurately."

Brian Cafferkey added: "Everything we buy to run the building is put on the system, so Beeline has helped us to develop a more disciplined approach to purchasing. Computer systems being as logical as they are there's no way of skimping the information required, and although it may seem to take longer initially the amount of time saved through reducing the risk of error is significant."

He continued: "At any time we can pull off reports for an overall picture of the financial situation. Already we've had a few surprises in certain areas, but we now have better information giving Esso the opportunity to negotiate more competitive prices from suppliers, resulting in considerable savings for the Company at the end of the day."

All telephone and local orders are being processed through Beeline, and the volume is growing fast. In December 100 orders worth £34,000 were placed and by mid-January confident use of the system had increased input to an additional 136 orders amounting to £40,000.

No-one is more aware of the move towards electronic data than senior information coordinator in Expro, Sally Jackson. But, surrounded by books and the mass of documents that make up the central file in the Expro library, Sally is not averse to the additional technology that Beeline supplies. "The transition to PROFS was smooth, so this new computer system was equally well accepted," she explained.

Sally feels that it is now only a matter of time before all the relevant records are on the system and the true benefits of Beeline will be felt. "It's definitely a better system for maintaining control over purchasing and accounts. It's more efficient for me having all order-related information easily accessible through one system."

The main function of Beeline for Sally's section is to order books and journals, but in the mail room at Victoria Street administration supervisor John Sweeney uses the system for dealing more with services rather than goods.

Ordering international courier services for all departments throughout Esso House (although some departments apparently still 'do their own thing!') John said of Beeline: "It helps us define the best service by identifying which firm can deliver the goods in the time required at the right price."

WHAT WOULD YOU SAY?

SECRETARIAL PROCEDURES

4.1 Correspondence to the Exxon Corporation in America is sent by electronic mail. What is electronic mail and how does it operate?

4.2 Nicola has to work overtime on occasions. Discuss the reasons why this is necessary and suggest some possible ways of reducing the amount of overtime required.

4.3 What sources of information would you expect Nicola to use in her job? What information obtainable from Viewdata could assist her?

4.4 Security of people at Esso is controlled from the Reception Office. How do you think Nicola controls the security of information in her office?

STRUCTURE OF BUSINESS

4.5 How does a rise in the price of oil affect the country's balance of payments?

4.6 What do you understand by the following:
(*a*) ordinary shareholder
(*b*) preference shareholder
(*c*) ultimate shareholder, eg Exxon Corporation
(*d*) holding company, eg Esso UK plc
(*e*) limited company, eg Esso Exploration and Production UK Ltd

4.7 Esso's petrol station shops retail a wide range of goods. How would a decision be made to determine which goods should be offered for sale?

4.8 What are the functions of the managing director of a company such as Esso Exploration and Production UK Ltd (*a*) in relation to the shareholders and (*b*) in the day-to-day operation of the company?

SECRETARIAL ADMINISTRATION

4.9 Draw up a check list for scheduling and organising meetings which Nicola can give to the secretary covering her work when she is absent on holiday.

4.10 Nicola's Managers do not always keep her fully informed of appointments which they make themselves, potentially causing additional work for her in rearranging appointments. How would you advise her to improve this situation?

4.11 An important meeting to be chaired by the Technical Manager has been arranged for 1000. Mr Docherty, who normally arrives at 0830, has not arrived by 0945 and no message to explain his absence has been received. What should Nicola do in these circumstances?

4.12 Why do you think the Technical Manager looks for 'impeccable interpersonal skills' in his secretary? What interpersonal skills are desirable in executive secretaries?

MANAGEMENT APPRECIATION

4.13 In a company as large as Esso it is important to establish good channels of communication. The company has the magazine *Newsline* and uses modern technology for communication between departments and companies. There is an on-going awareness for staff involvement and participation to aid motivation. Your manager is aware of quality circles and asks you to review this technique and advise him of your views on this and any other similar ideas for your company. Prepare a report on your findings, conclusions and recommendations.

4.14 Planning features greatly in the work of all managers and you are often called upon to use such terms as 'corporate', 'tactical', 'operational' and 'strategic'. Mr Docherty is to speak on a Management Short Course and has asked you to prepare some notes for him explaining these planning terms, which will be the basis of a handout for the short course delegates.

4.15 Esso develops the qualities of effective leadership within the managerial hierarchy. Outline the roles and differing styles of leadership likely to be encountered in the company.

4.16 In some areas of its operation Esso has Industrial Relations Advisers. What benefits do you foresee in employing such advisers and how would their role and functions differ from Personnel Advisers?

ADDITIONAL STUDENT LEARNING ACTIVITIES

FIND OUT

More about Esso UK plc and two other major oil companies in the UK – state:

- their registered addresses
- directors' names
- sales turnover
- capital structure

ROLE PLAY

A brief talk to a group of college students visiting Esso explaining how the company has computerised its office procedures and comparing these with the manual methods which were used in a small firm where you worked before joining Esso.

Manville Limited, builders

This case study focuses on the secretarial role of Kate Lovegrove who is employed by Manville Limited, a small private firm specialising in quality building services such as extensions, alterations, restoration work and re-furbishment of buildings.

BACKGROUND

The firm began in 1977 when Mr Burville and Mr Waterman decided to work together with their wives to establish a building business. Mr Water-man had been working on his own for about two years since being employed as an engineer in a local firm. The work during these two years involved various sub-contracting building tasks for local firms and Mr Burville lent a hand, on a part-time basis, to assist Mr Waterman in preparing drawings and estimates. Mr Burville, a trained carpenter, had assumed responsibility with his firm for estimating and surveying. Mr Waterman's work expanded rapidly until it became necessary to take on a full-time partner. Mr Burville decided to leave his firm and join Mr Waterman on a full-time basis and they formed a private limited company called Manville Limited. Mr Waterman's wife was appointed company secretary with responsibility for arranging meetings of the directors and for the accountancy work. The firm quickly established itself in the locality and as the work increased so did the number of people it employed. It now employs sixteen people as detailed in the organisation chart on page 37. Sub-contractors are engaged for such tasks as plastering, electrical installation and heating.

Premises

The firm moved into modern premises in a shopping precinct a year ago and ventured into the retail trade by offering paint for sale, but after a trial period of six months they found the turnover too slow and decided to discontinue this line of business. There is an open-plan office (with a reception area) which is occupied by Mrs Waterman, Kate Lovegrove, Joanna Brinton and the office junior. The Chairman (Mr Burville) has a separate office so that he can receive clients, sub-contractors, etc, in private.

THE SECRETARY'S ROLE AND FUNCTIONS

Kate Lovegrove is secretary to the directors and in this capacity assumes responsibility for the general running of the office. She also has an important public relations role for the firm in receiving callers, handling telephone enquiries and communicating with clients during the course of a building project. Some callers are not always welcome as evidenced by the notice on the front of Kate's desk: 'We shoot every third salesman – the second one just left!'. Kate occupies an important position which involves using her own initiative and being responsible for the office when Mrs Waterman is away. She has been with the firm for over two years and had previously worked in a variety of secretarial and clerical capacities including a clerical position with the area health authority where her work was less varied and there were fewer opportunities to meet people. Her job at Manville covers most aspects of running a small office, such as typing correspondence and business documents; audio-typing; composing letters from notes; reception; telephoning; filing; using a copier; arranging appointments for directors and keeping their diaries; receiving and despatching mail; preparing advertisements; ordering and controlling stationery; and the training and supervision of the office junior. Kate uses an electronic typewriter and is preparing to use a recently purchased microcomputer for word processing and documentation. Since she makes visits on behalf of the firm, Kate is allocated a company car. The files are kept in vertical filing cabinets and classified alphabetically by clients' names which are cross-referenced to their numbers on client index cards. Estimates (*see* specimen on page 38) are filed numerically in a current project file and any estimates not accepted are transferred to a 'dead' file after six months.

Kate has been given the task of filling a vacancy for a new office junior and training the successful applicant in Manville's methods. She has placed an advertisement in the local paper as follows:

'Office Junior urgently required by Local Builder – Friendly Company – Varied duties – Apply Manville Ltd, 12 The Precinct, Winchester Road, Chandlers Ford, Hants S02 2GB.'

Five replies have been received (*see* pages 40 to 43). Another applicant, Anne Billingham, telephoned to say that she was interested in the vacancy, but wondered whether she was too old at 20. At present she works as a cashier at a supermarket but she likes the idea of working in an office. She studied typing at school and passed a Pitman Elementary Typing examination in it. Kate, who received the telephone call, noted that Anne had an excellent telephone manner. The office junior will be required to assist both Kate and Joanna and undertake their duties when they are absent for holidays or sickness. It is intended that the new employee will also be responsible for handling telephone calls.

Kate enjoys the personal contacts with clients but dislikes the task of reminding them when payment of their account is overdue.

Wages

The wages for the employees are prepared manually by Mrs Waterman and are paid weekly through the bank's auto-pay system. A computerised system is currently under consideration and Mrs Waterman has to be satisfied that it will prove beneficial for a payroll of less than 20 employees.

OFFICE PROCEDURE FOR A BUILDING JOB

The following is the office procedure used by Manvilles for the administration of a building job, in this case the construction of a bay window, from the time an enquiry is received to the receipt of payment for work undertaken.

1 Request received to supply an estimate for building a bay window.
2 Complete an estimate request form.
3 Telephone to arrange an appointment for Mr Burville to visit the client's premises to assess the task.
4 Mr Burville drafts an estimate which is typed and a copy filed in a current project file.
5 If the estimate is acceptable to the client an estimate acceptance form is sent for completion.
6 The job is entered in the estimate acceptances book.
7 A file is opened for the client and a job number allocated to it.
8 Planning application forms are completed, where applicable.
9 A work progress chart is prepared.
10 Letter sent to client thanking him/her for the order and indicating an approximate date for commencement of work.
11 A job card is completed for Mr Waterman.
12 The job is entered on the work programme display board.
13 A client's index card is prepared.
14 File passed to Mr Burville for ordering materials.
15 Orders typed.
16 If sub-contractors are required, orders are typed.
17 Telephone client to confirm date of commencement of work.
18 Throughout the work the secretary keeps the client informed of any sub-contractors visiting their premises.
19 When the work is completed Mr Burville gives the secretary details of costs and an invoice is typed.
20 Invoice is entered in an invoice book.
21 Copies of the invoice are distributed as follows:

   (a) Client's file
   (b) Company Secretary
   (c) Accounts Clerk.

22 Accounts Clerk keeps the copy invoices in a sales file and enters the transaction in the sales ledger.

23 If no payment is received within seven days of the date of the invoice, a
letter requesting immediate payment is sent. This practice is essential to
provide adequate cash flow for the payment of wages, which are paid
weekly.

24 When payment is made the secretary prepares a paying-in slip and pays
the cheque into the bank, marking off the relevant invoice.

25 The payment is entered in the sales ledger by the accounts clerk.

26 A courtesy letter is sent to the client thanking him/her for the cheque and
the job.

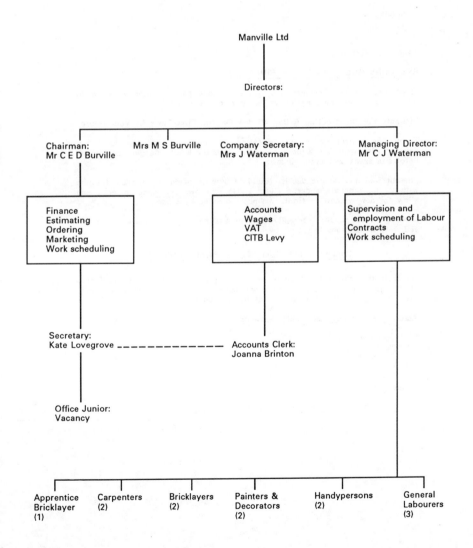

Manville Ltd
The Complete Building Service

12 The Precinct Winchester Road Chandlers Ford Hampshire SO2 2GB

Telephone: (0703) 263438

Established since 1977

Our Ref: CEDB/KML
Est. 1646

Mrs. J. Harrison,
"Trelawne",
Southdown Road,
Shawford,
NR. WINCHESTER,
Hants.

14th July, 19

Dear Mrs. Harrison,

RE: CONSTRUCTION OF BAY WINDOW.

Thank you for your enquiry and further to our visit we have pleasure in submitting our estimate as follows for your consideration:

Estimate For Constructing A Bay Window On The First Floor Of Your House

To provide scaffolding to rear elevation and take out and remove 2 No. existing windows. Set aside for reuse. Strip back tile hanging and check lintol size spans over both windows.

Cut out wall and remove debris. Build in purpose made bay window framing with 2 No. brackets under. Refix 2 No. windows set aside in ends and allow for new window to front. (Window supplied by others).

Make good to plaster internally, reform tile hanging and leave ready for your own decoration.

THIS FOR THE SUM OF £2,889.70 PLUS VAT

We trust that this estimate will meet with your approval and included free of charge is the preparation of plans upon acceptance. (Local Authority Fees are payable direct by the client to the Council).

Assuring you of our continued attention.

Yours sincerely,
for MANVILLE LTD.,

C.E.D. Burville,
DIRECTOR.

For Terms and Conditions please see reverse of page.

Directors: C. J. Waterman C. E. D. Burville M. S. Burville J. Waterman and Secretary.   Registered in England Reg. No. 1316226   VAT No. 293 5709 26

EXISTING REAR ELEVATION.

Letter 1

49 Milford Square
Chandlers Ford
SO23 2UY

2 July 19-

Manville Ltd
Chandlers Ford

Dear Sirs,

Your advertisement in the Evening News interests me as I wish to gain experience to become an accountant.

I am 17 years of age with GCSE exams in five subjects including English and Mathematics and I am at present studying for the BTEC National Certificate. I work in an engineering company at Windlesham, but I find that the travelling takes too long and is too expensive. My home is near to your office and it would be more convenient for me to work for you.

I shall be pleased to be considered for your vacancy.

Yours faithfully

Robin Cook

<u>Letter 2</u>

13 Burlington Place
Romsey
SO23 2OT

1 July 19—

Manville Ltd
12 The Precinct
Winchester Road
Chandlers Ford
Hants
SO2 2GB

Dear Sir

With reference to your vacancy for an office junior
advertised in last night's Evening News I wish to
be considered for it.

I am 17 years of age and have recently completed
a full-time course at the College of Further Education
for the BTEC First Diploma. The course covered a
wide range of office subjects including Office Practice,
Communication, Numeracy, Finance, Information Processing,
Keyboarding, Information Transcription and Receptionist/
Telephonist Duties. During the course I also gained
work experience in the office of a local estate agent
which I enjoyed very much.

I would be very interested in working for a building
firm and, if selected, I shall be pleased to attend
for interview.

Yours faithfully

Jane Snowden.

Letter 3

123 Southgate Way
Eastleigh
Hants
SO5 8AW

2 July 19-

For the attention of the Personnel Manager
Manville Ltd
12 The Precinct
Chandlers Ford
SO2 2GB

Dear Sir

I wish to make application for your vacancy advertised in the
Evening News.

During the last two years I have been studying secretarial
subjects at a private secretarial college. I was prepared for
the LCCI Private Secretary's Certificate examination which I took
last month and I already have RSA certificates for Shorthand (80
wpm); Typewriting (Stage III); Audio-Typing (Stage II); Word
Processing (Stage II) and Secretarial Duties (Stage II). I can
write shorthand at 100 wpm and am looking forward to using this
skill in my work.

I hope you will consider my application for your vacancy.

Yours faithfully

K F RAVAL (Miss)

Letter 4

19 St John's Road
Chandlers Ford

Dear Mr Manville

I saw your advert in the paper and my
mum said I should write to you as the
job looks intresting.
I did YTS but left it because the colledge
course didn't work out very well. So I
haven't got a job now and I do badly
need the money.
My boyfriend, Tim, Blake, works for your
firm and it would be ever so nice if
I could to.
Hope to here from you soon!
Yours Faithfully

Mandy Clarke

Letter 5

88 Market Street
Eastleigh
Hants
SO5 2VH

1 July 19-

Manville Ltd.
12 The Precinct
Winchester Road
Chandlers Ford
Hants
SO2 2GB

Dear Sirs,

I am writing in reply to your advertisement in this evening's paper as I am interested in obtaining an office job.

I have just completed my school education at the local comprehensive school and have taken six GCSE subjects. My teachers expect me to be awarded good grades, especially in English and Mathematics. Although I have not studied Business Studies at school, I do intend to take evening classes or preferably a day-release course at the local college in Typing and Accounts so that I can make good progress in an office career.

I am available to commence work immediately and I shall be pleased to be considered for your vacancy.

Yours faithfully

Fiona Walker

YOUR VIEWS ARE REQUIRED

SECRETARIAL PROCEDURES

5.1 When an office junior is appointed she/he will be expected to handle the opening and sorting of incoming mail and the preparation and posting of outgoing mail. Write notes of guidance on these tasks to assist the new employee.

5.2 Kate Lovegrove's light-hearted 'threat' to salesmen was meant to deter the many representatives who call without appointment and invariably waste her time and interrupt her busy schedule. Suggest how you would handle such callers to minimise the time involved. How would you differentiate between the callers whose services/goods might be beneficial to the firm and those who have nothing to contribute?

5.3 State the business documents which will pass between Manvilles and their clients, from the receipt of an enquiry to the payment for work undertaken. Explain the purpose of each document.

5.4 Wages are paid by the bank's 'auto-pay' system. What is this system and how does it benefit the employees and the employer?

STRUCTURE OF BUSINESS

5.5 Mr Waterman and Mr Burville formed a private limited company. Why do you think they chose this type of business organisation? What are the major differences between a partnership and a private limited company?

5.6 What do you understand by 'turnover'? Why do you think there was a slow turnover in the sale of paint and how might this have been rectified?

5.7 How is Manville Ltd influenced or directed as a result of the decisions of central and local government?

5.8 What are the chief risks that the directors of Manville Ltd might wish to insure against?

SECRETARIAL ADMINISTRATION

5.9 How would you advise Kate Lovegrove in her preparation to use the new microcomputer for word processing and documentation? What aspects of her work could be computerised?

5.10 Draw up a job description and a job specification for the new office junior. How would these assist in making the new appointment?

5.11 Examine the replies received to the advertisement for an office junior and suggest, with reasons, which of the applicants should be called for an interview.

5.12 Most of the forms in use at Manvilles are typed by Kate. What basic principles of good form design should she use in this work?

MANAGEMENT APPRECIATION

5.13 If the new office junior proved to be unsatisfactory, what arrangements should be made for his/her dismissal having regard to current legislation and what steps could be taken to avoid employing unsatisfactory staff in the future?

5.14 Design an internal training programme for the office junior and suggest any external courses which would be appropriate.

5.15 Is a computerised wages system beneficial for a payroll of less than 20 employees? Advise Mrs Waterman.

5.16 Manvilles require payment of invoices within seven days and systematically follow up any clients who fail to pay, in order to maintain an adequate cash flow. What further action might be taken to minimise cash flow difficulties and establish an effective debt collection system?

ADDITIONAL STUDENT LEARNING ACTIVITIES

FIND OUT

what stationery supplies Kate Lovegrove should stock in her stationery cupboard and what quantities should be maintained for each item.

ROLE PLAY

a tactful telephone conversation with a client who has failed to pay an account by the due date.

IBM UK Limited

BACKGROUND

As you would expect from a company engaged in the development, manufacture, marketing and servicing of information-handling products, services and supplies, this case study specialises in the use of new technology. IBM produces electronic typewriters, telecommunications systems and services and information processors ranging from personal computers to large mainframe computers. The company plays a leading role in the technology industry which continues to be exciting and strategically important for the United Kingdom's economy and prosperity.

IBM UK Ltd was formed in 1951 with sales offices in London and a factory in Scotland. Shortly afterwards offices were opened in a number of major cities throughout Britain. It is a private company which is wholly owned by IBM UK Holdings Ltd, a subsidiary of IBM Corporation, New York, USA. The company decided to move its headquarters out of London to Portsmouth in 1970 and it now employs about 3000 people there in modern purpose-built buildings. Sharing the headquarters is one of IBM's international centres which has three major responsibilities: to develop information systems for use by other national IBM companies; to provide and maintain international data bases of IBM information which can be used in Europe and elsewhere in the world; and to run an internal telecommunications network that keeps information flowing between IBM branch offices and manufacturing plants throughout Europe.

DIRECTOR'S RESPONSIBILITIES

The secretary featured in this case study is Mrs Vivienne Coleshill who is private secretary to the Resident Director for IBM in Hampshire – Mr John Huffell – who is based at Head Office and operates within the Personnel Department. The organisation chart on page 49 shows the structure of the company's hierarchy and the positions of John Huffell and Vivienne Coleshill in it.

Mr Huffell is responsible for the following:

- managing IBM's locations in Portsmouth, including the health and safety of employees

- overseeing the location managers' programme throughout the UK
- managing IBM's 'face' with the community in Hampshire including sponsorships, donations, charities, education, etc
- reviewing matters arising from the 'open door' policy

Some of the terms used in these responsibilities may be unfamiliar to you and brief explanations are, therefore, given. IBM's 'face' with the community is its commitment to good corporate citizenship through long-term, planned and carefully implemented community support programmes embracing education, job creation, sponsorship and the secondment of IBM employees. For example IBM supports the Youth Training Scheme; social responsibility programmes for conservation, environment, the Third World and the disadvantaged; information technology centres; and sponsorship of a wide range of cultural events. The 'open door' policy is one which allows employees to have freedom of access to their managers, and an employee wishing to appeal against a manager's decision may take the matter to middle or senior management for review.

SECRETARY'S RESPONSIBILITIES

Vivienne Coleshill's job description takes the form of a performance plan (*see* page 50), which she prepares in liaison with her manager, specifying her job objectives and performance criteria. Once a year her manager records on this form his assessment of her attainment and rating, having regard to the performance criteria and this then forms the basis for her personal development plan highlighting any staff development and training programmes necessary to enhance her career and work effectiveness.

Vivienne is fortunate to have the facility to communicate electronically with her colleagues in any part of the IBM organisation in the UK as well as abroad via the National Office Support System (NOSS). She uses it for sending and receiving electronic mail, keeping her director's diary, scheduling meetings, word processing, filing and looking up information from a centralised data base. Most IBM employees now use NOSS as part of their daily routine and it is estimated to have increased productivity by 12 per cent. Vivienne still finds an electronic typewriter useful for small tasks, such as addressing envelopes and labels, typing notes and messages on compliment slips. She has access to fax, telex and copier facilities which are housed near to her office. Although the computerised office system provides useful access to data there is still a need for papers to be kept in conventional filing cabinets. Her files are classified by subject and kept for as long as is necessary, but most categories of correspondence are kept no longer than two years. A travel agent and a bank operate within Head Office to provide a comprehensive range of services for secretaries. Photocopies of street plans or railway timetables suitably highlighted are normally sufficient for itineraries. A 'clean desk' policy is in operation, controlled by security guards, to ensure strict security of information and a system of passwords is used to safeguard computerised data. The secretaries serve as hostesses at IBM

Vivienne Coleshill in her 'automated' office at IBM UK Ltd.

sponsored events, such as concerts and exhibitions. Vivienne considers her most important task is to relieve her director by helping to remove the stress from his daily routine and to handle much of the detail involved in location management. With the large volume of work and complexities of the job it is not always possible for tasks to be completed when required or for people to be reached immediately, which create problems and frustration for both Vivienne and her director.

Many of Vivienne's contacts are in education and in other academic and cultural spheres outside the IBM organisation and, in order to assist her employer when he is involved with such meetings as TVE, Governors, Community Projects, etc, she has to try to understand their methods and organisational structures. She intends to assemble important details about these contacts with the outside world to provide a quick means of reference in her office.

The secretary's daily routine

Vivienne's daily routine has to be as flexible as possible to enable her to respond quickly to constantly changing needs and priorities. If her director has a meeting early in the day she also arrives early to prepare for it. At the beginning of each day she supplies the director with the papers and files required for the day's business. In turn he dictates notes from the previous day's work which she uses to compose letters and memos and to conduct telephone conversations. The diary is planned with some 'keep free' time to allow the director and secretary to liaise with each other. The secretary opens and reads the incoming mail and decides which items the director must see, which items she can deal with herself and which items should be re-directed to others. The final collection of mail is made at 1615 but if Vivienne has any letters which must be despatched after this time, she stamps them, using her own stamp supply and posts them on the way home.

Meetings

When Vivienne is required to call a meeting for her director she uses NOSS to find a suitable date for all participants and to notify them of the meeting. She enters the period within which the meeting is required; time of day; expected duration; venue; nature of business to be discussed; and the names of the participants. The diaries of each of the participants are accessed, a suitable date is revealed and notices are distributed to all concerned by electronic mail. In addition to convening the meeting, Vivienne books the meeting room, orders refreshments, allocates a time in the director's diary for preparation, takes notes at the meeting, prepares draft minutes for approval by the chairman and finally distributes the minutes to the participants.

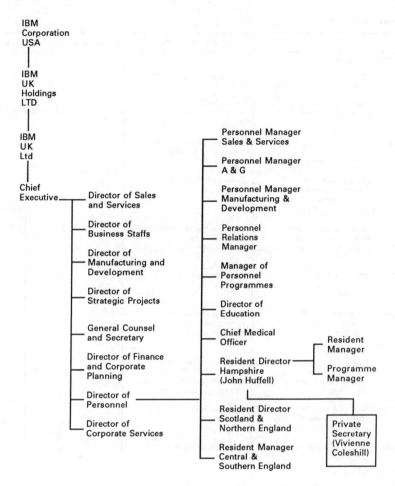

An Extract from the IBM Organisation Chart

Performance Plan

Objective	Performance Criteria	Notes on Attainment	Rating
1 COMMUNICATION			
1.1 Ensure a polite and clear telephone manner	No complaints on manner and attitude		
1.2 Where possible ensure messages are clearly understood	No important misunderstandings		
1.3 Use systems, eg NOSS, to effect internal correspondence	Same day transfer of notes and messages where possible		
1.4 Ensure timely and accurate turnaround of typed letters	Same day completion where possible		
2 PLANNING			
2.1 Maintain up-to-date diaries and plan to minimise last minute changes	Avoid rearrangements due to over-run and non-attendance		
2.2 Ensure effective preparation for meetings and discussions	Avoid last minute preparation		
2.3 Administer an effective system of bring/up and follow/up	Timely responses to all requests and required action		
3 ADMINISTRATION			
3.1 Establish budget and monitor expenditure highlighting potential out of line situations	Timely identification of potential problems to allow alternative corrective actions		
3.2 Meet the requirements of the company's safety and security policies	No violations		
3.3 Set up and maintain a secretarial will*	Up-to-date record		
4 ADDED VALUE			
4.1 Advise on systems usage	Maintain state of the art usage as appropriate		
4.2 Handle correspondence and queries to the limit of knowledge and ability to research	Avoidance of passing on correspondence that could have been previously cleared		
4.3 Ensure that activities such as correspondence and presentations are of the highest quality	No errors and consistency of presentation format		
5 PERSONAL DEVELOPMENT			
5.1 Increase knowledge of external bodies and local and national issues	Demonstrate knowledge through increased added value		
5.2 Learn PC/NOSS applications to develop efficient system usage	Maintain state of the art knowledge		

* A 'secretarial will' is a secretary's personal data file containing essential details about the manager; his/her preferences; check-lists; office procedures; use of forms; distribution lists; etc, as a guide to a replacement secretary when required for cover or when a successor is appointed.

QUESTION TIME

SECRETARIAL PROCEDURES

6.1 What services would you expect the travel agent and the bank to provide for you as a secretary at IBM?

6.2 Explain what is meant by a 'clean desk' policy and prepare a code of practice to ensure security of information.

6.3 How would you suggest that Vivienne could 'remove the stress from her employer's daily routine'?

6.4 Your employer's attainment assessment of Objective 2.3 in your performance plan – administer an effective system of bring/up and follow/up – states: 'Some important matters overlooked'. Suggest an efficient follow-up procedure and explain how it would improve your performance.

STRUCTURE OF BUSINESS

6.5 Why do you think the technology industry is described as 'exciting and strategically important for the United Kingdom's economy and prosperity'?

6.6 The IBM International Centre provides a telecommunication network between branch offices and manufacturing plants throughout Europe. Discuss the role of the EC in facilitating UK trade connections with other European countries.

6.7 The Resident Director is Chairman of the local TVE Committee involving the local authority and heads of schools. Why is industry involved in TVE? In what ways do the organisation and financing of the local authority differ from those of IBM?

6.8 What are the major differences between a private joint-stock company (such as IBM) and a public joint-stock company? Consider their formation, organisation and control.

SECRETARIAL ADMINISTRATION

6.9 How would you advise Vivienne to assemble important details about her contacts with the outside world? Suggest what details she should record.

6.10 List the items you would include in your 'secretarial will' (full-time students should use one of the case studies in this book as the basis for their answer). Explain how you would compile it and where you would keep it.

6.11 Prepare the objectives and performance criteria for your performance plan, as illustrated on page 50. In what ways does a performance plan differ from a job description?

6.12 Why is it not always possible for tasks to be completed when required and for people to be contacted immediately? Suggest how Vivienne might be able to minimise these problems and frustrations.

MANAGEMENT APPRECIATION

6.13 Discuss the impact of new technology on management at IBM. There is still a need for papers to be kept in conventional filing cabinets. Why is it that the paperless office has not yet been achieved?

6.14 Why do you think IBM has an 'open door' policy? Are there any disadvantages in using this method of communication?

6.15 IBM moved its headquarters from London to Portsmouth in 1970. What factors would have influenced the company in making this move?

6.16 IBM attached a great deal of importance to its 'face' with the community and the contributions it makes through corporate responsibility programmes – resulting in considerable financial commitments. Why is this? Would IBM be more profitable if it devoted these resources to reducing the price of its products?

ADDITIONAL STUDENT LEARNING ACTIVITIES

The IBM Corporation of USA is a multi-national company with a subsidiary company in the UK

FIND OUT

what other major foreign companies operate in the UK and what goods or services they provide.

ROLE PLAY

a hostess/secretary serving at an IBM sponsored concert with an accompanying commentary on dress, shoes, etc – to take the form of a mini-fashion show.

The Industrial Society

INTRODUCTION

It is appropriate to include the Industrial Society in a book of case studies for secretaries as it specialises in organising courses and conferences – a task which secretaries are often called upon to undertake. In addition, the secretary should be aware of the services of the Industrial Society so that these can be utilised when required.

SERVICES OF THE INDUSTRIAL SOCIETY

The Industrial Society, which is self-financing and non-profit making, aims to help organisations to become more effective; more productive; more profitable; more customer orientated; and to have a more highly committed and motivated workforce. It helps to spread good practices needed to achieve employee involvement by running training courses and conferences on employee-related issues and by advising and assisting organisations in all sectors, from industrial and commercial organisations to public services. The Society has 16 000 member organisations, including major trade unions, for which it offers the following services:

- **Leadership training** – instructing and advising managers at every level in the skills of managing people
- **Communication and consultation** – helping organisations to install effective communication systems such as team briefing, quality circles, suggestion schemes, and consultative committees
- **Productive management/union relations** – training and advising managers and union officers in how to make their relationships at the workplace productive
- **Conditions of employment** – advising on pension schemes, hours of work, catering, employment, etc
- **Young people** – helping organisations to ensure that their young people are trained for the future
- **Achieving recognition of why industry matters** – co-operating with

schools, universities and community organisations to promote an understanding of why industry matters

- **Courses and conferences** – organising a wide range of residential and non-residential courses and conferences dealing with such topics as Secretarial Development, Computers and Information Technology, Industrial Relations, Management Training and Leadership, Supervisor Training and Leadership, Communication Skills, Conditions of Employment and other specialist areas
- **In-house training** – offering 'tailor-made' courses, specific to individual training requirements
- **Information service** – providing information on any matters relating to employing people, including legislation, policies and procedures
- **Publications** – publishing a wide range of short, practical books on management skills, employment legislation, industrial relations, employee communication and consultation and communication skills. A range of videos is available which can be incorporated into training programmes. A newsletter, *Briefing* is published monthly providing up-to-date information on courses, special events and conferences. A magazine is published quarterly and is designed to keep managers up-to-date with good practice in managing people at work
- **Surveys and audits** – undertaking surveys and audits in many organisations, particularly in the field of industrial relations and employee communication. The surveys are followed by findings and recommendations on what future actions the organisations should consider taking

Topics under discussion

At the time of going to press a selection of the topics under discussion in the Industrial Society training sessions included:

- **Promoting good relations**. Industrial relations have changed and developed over recent years – horizons have broadened and while the traditional image of management and union in confrontation still exists, managers and unions are now working together, breaking new ground for the benefit of employees and the organisation. A variety of courses and seminars on this theme are offered
- **Profit from care**. A seminar identifying customers' needs and creating a system which is responsive to them and the changing market place, resulting in greater profitability
- **Working women in the 1990s**. It has been forecast that by the year 2000 only half the workforce will have full-time jobs. This workshop looked at the likely patterns of work in the next decade and considered how women working in industry and education could develop the skills they would need
- **Is anyone there?** A seminar for those responsible for ensuring that the telephone is used to the maximum benefit of the organisation
- **Acting against alcohol**. Despite losses to industry of £2 billion each year through drink-related problems, few senior managers have recognised the

scale of the problem or considered how to deal with it. Drink-related problems do not only affect alcoholics – colleagues and ultimately an organisation's profitability suffer as the standard of work deteriorates. This conference identified the symptoms of alcoholism and suggested methods of dealing with the difficulties caused by drink

- **Delegation**. In order to obtain the best possible results from their team, managers and supervisors need to make the best use of the time, skill and commitment of their subordinates. Effective delegation is essential to achieving this end and this course is designed to develop the ability to delegate
- **Meetings: chairing and participating**. A course designed to help those who chair formal or informal meetings to make meetings shorter and more productive; to have clear guidelines for the preparation and structure of meetings; and to apply the skills of leadership and control of meetings
- **Meeting the media**. A workshop to help the participants to face a media interview (television or radio) armed with the knowledge that they can present their case with conviction and equanimity
- **Senior secretary in management today**. A course which enables senior secretaries and personal assistants to understand the responsibilities of management and provide a high standard of administrative support; be able to ensure that the departmental and organisation communication works effectively; be able to take minutes and draw up agenda for meetings; and obtain up-to-date knowledge of current office systems

CASE STUDY SETTING

The setting for this study is the Southern England Office of the Industrial Society and the work of Anne Douglas, the Area Administrator and Secretary to the Area Manager. Her position in the organisation is shown in the extract of the accountability chart given on page 57. Anne is responsible for two secretaries and other occasional temporary staff who serve as course administrators for the management advisers. Relevant extracts from Anne's job description (page 58) indicate the key areas in her work. The secretaries use electronic typewriters and a word processor and are required to type reports from management advisers which are sometimes handwritten and not always easy to interpret. An electronic telephone system has been installed, a feature of which is the playing of computerised tunes to callers while they wait to be connected. Anne has a heavy workload and there are times when it is difficult to avoid a backlog of work. Meeting 'deadlines' can often mean working late in the evenings. Anne recognises the need and desirability of delegating work, but is aware that it is time consuming in the short term. An additional dimension raised by Anne is the provision of a secretarial support service for the Associate Adviser who works from home and calls in at the office once a month. The remoteness of an adviser working away from the office can create difficulties, especially with communication but this situation may become increasingly common with the emergence of the 'paperless office'.

Communications

Regular meetings are held in all departments to communicate and consult with staff. All staff attend monthly departmental briefing meetings when Heads of Department discuss administrative matters as well as the Society's progress and new policies. Staff are also informed of staff news, organisational changes and social events in a weekly circular which is distributed to all offices in the Society. Anne encourages her staff to attend courses for their own self development and also where she identifies a specific training need for their immediate job requirements.

THE ORGANISATION OF COURSES AND CONFERENCES

The organisation of courses, conferences, seminars, workshops, working lunches, etc is a major task for secretaries employed at the Industrial Society. Checklists of essential steps to be taken are provided for the guidance of secretaries covering the following:

- **Programme** Title/content
  Drafting/approval
  Printing/proof reading
  Distribution
  Publicity – internal
         – external

- **Venue** Select and book accommodation
  Catering arrangements:
     morning coffee
     sherry
     lunch
     afternoon tea
  Cloakroom facilities
  Flowers
  Direction signs
  Confirm final numbers

- **Speakers** Invitation/appointment
  Send programme
  Travel arrangements
  Hotel accommodation
  Equipment requirements
  Letter of thanks with fee

- **Financial** Calculate course/conference fee
  Determine minimum number of delegates required for
     viability
  Check for viability of bookings
  Record/bank receipts
  Record/prepare cheques for expenses

- **Aids**   Order: microphones
                          lectern
                          projector and screen
                          tape/video recorder
                  Set up equipment
                  Return equipment to supplier

- **Delegates**   List of names and companies
                  Folders
                  Badges
                  Hosting arrangements

- **Literature** Book stand
  (if required)   Order forms
                  Invoice for books ordered

- **Press**   Invitations
  (if required)   Press release
                  Table

- **Staff**   Briefing
                  Prepare staff accountability
                  Debriefing

The Industrial Society

Accountability chart

South East Area

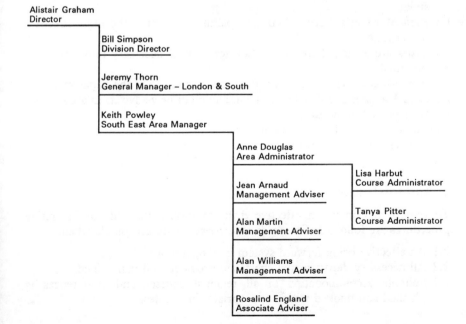

JOB DESCRIPTION (extract)

Anne Douglas

Job title: Area Administrator
Department: South East Region
Responsible to: Area Manager
Overall objectives: To promote the work of the Industrial Society by providing an efficient and effective secretarial and financial information back-up to the Area Manager.

To ensure a satisfactory administrative back-up for advisers by the supervision and co-ordination of the work of the secretaries/course administrators.

KEY AREAS

1 Secretarial

To provide a high standard of secretarial service for the Area Manager. *Standards of performance* are acceptable when:

1.1 All correspondence is answered either by phone or letter within 24 hours of receipt or referred to Area Manager within 24 hours for identification of action;
1.2 All typed work is accurate and visually pleasing in accordance with house style;
1.3 Area Manager's diary is kept and planned to ensure the most effective use of time;
1.4 Visits are arranged for Area Manager and all necessary information is provided;
1.5 Area Manager is assisted with the general running of the department;
1.6 Area Manager is assisted with the induction of new advisers in accordance with procedure notes;
1.7 Matters which affect the administration of the department are discussed and resolved at Heads of Department meetings.

2 Administration

To prepare and maintain effective drills to ensure that all administrative procedures are followed. *Standards of performance* are acceptable when:

2.1 An effective bring forward system is in operation;
2.2 All necessary departmental charts are provided and maintained;
2.3 Suitable accommodation of all regional courses and conferences is planned and booked within appropriate time scales.

3 Management

To recruit, train and maintain morale of the department's team of secretaries/ course administrators. *To be responsible* for monitoring and organising the secretaries' workload. *To be responsible* for the secretaries/course administrators' performance in supporting their advisers. *Standards of performance* are acceptable when:

3.1 An induction/training plan for 'new secretaries is planned prior to their arrival and fully briefed on Day 1 – in accordance with procedure notes;

3.2 All course administration and other secretarial tasks are allocated fairly amongst the team;

3.3 All secretaries have a job description and up-to-date targets which include a personal development target. Targets to be discussed at least every four months;

3.4 All appraisals are carried out by the due date and appraisal forms completed and passed to appropriate advisers for completion within 48 hours of appraisal;

3.5 Team meetings are held monthly;

3.6 1:1 interviews with secretaries are held at least monthly;

3.7 Course and conference routines, including associated paperwork, are followed, due dates are met and programmes printed accurately and on time;

3.8 Disciplinary and complaint procedures are dealt with fairly and in accordance with procedure notes.

4 Financial

To prepare and maintain records for the department in accordance with budgetary requirements. *Standards of performance* are acceptable when:

4.1 All departmental expenses are entered in the appropriate books within 5 days of receipt;

4.2 End of month returns are completed in accordance with procedure notes;

4.3 Forward loadings and income projections are compiled accurately;

4.4 Petty cash and luncheon voucher procedures are administered accurately;

4.5 All financial records are maintained in a neat and orderly manner.

14.04.--

PROBLEM PAGE

SECRETARIAL PROCEDURES

7.1 Regular appraisal interviews are conducted at the Industrial Society. How do these benefit the Society and the employee? What matters should be included in an appraisal interview?

7.2 Some Management Advisers spend their valuable time writing out their reports for typing and the secretaries experience some difficulties in interpreting their handwriting. Draft a memo for Anne Douglas to send to her Manager suggesting alternative methods which would save time for both advisers and secretaries when producing reports.

7.3 What facilities would you expect to be provided on the electronic telephone system? Is it beneficial for callers to be 'entertained' by music when they need to hold on? What techniques would you advise the telephonist to adopt in order to enhance this computerised musical communication?

7.4 One of the Management Advisers is retiring after 15 years' service with the Industrial Society. You are asked to arrange an informal buffet lunch for him and his wife. Prepare a timetable to ensure that the arrangements are carried out in a logical order for a successful social occasion.

STRUCTURE OF BUSINESS

7.5 Why do you think the Industrial Society attaches importance to promoting an understanding of 'why industry matters'?

7.6 The Industrial Society offers a course entitled 'Drafting Personnel Policies and Procedures'. What topics would you expect to be covered in such a course? What steps should be taken to implement a new personnel policy?

7.7 Discuss how you would determine the price of a course.

7.8 The Industrial Society course 'Profit from Care' deals with systems which are responsive to customers' needs in the changing market place. What do you understand by 'the changing market place' and how would you be responsive to customers' needs?

SECRETARIAL ADMINISTRATION

7.9 Complete Anne Douglas's job description with two further key areas for: 5. Communication and 6. Personal development, and include appropriate objectives and standards of performance.

7.10 Suggest solutions to the problem of providing a secretarial support service for the Associate Adviser who works from home and only calls at the office once a month.

7.11 What advice would you give in the course 'Meetings: chairing and participating' to make meetings shorter and more productive?

7.12 Suggest a topic of current importance for senior secretaries which will be the theme for a two-day conference. Draw up a checklist for organising this conference showing the items to be dealt with at each of the following time intervals:

12 weeks before the conference
8 weeks before the conference
4 weeks before the conference
2 weeks before the conference
1 day before the conference
1st day of the conference
2nd day of the conference
After the conference

MANAGEMENT APPRECIATION

7.13 How would you advise Anne Douglas to manage her heavy workload? Is there a problem in delegating some of her non-routine work?

7.14 Explain how 'industrial relations have changed and developed over recent years'.

7.15 Discuss the importance of the Industrial Society's role in helping organisations to install effective communication systems. What are 'quality circles'? How practical or desirable is it to involve employees in the decision-making process?

7.16 What methods of dealing with the difficulties caused by drink would you consider making at the conference 'Acting against alcohol'?

ADDITIONAL STUDENT LEARNING ACTIVITIES

FIND OUT

the names, addresses and other relevant information concerning other organisations in the United Kingdom which offer training courses, publications and advice on management and employee-related issues.

ROLE PLAY

a discussion on patterns of work in the next decade and the effects they will have on the employment of women – as you would envisage it taking place in the Workshop 'Working Women in the 1990s'.

Abraham & Fothergil, Solicitors

BACKGROUND

Karen Simpkins is Secretary to Kenneth Winters, a senior partner in Abraham & Fothergil, a firm of solicitors in Winton city centre. The firm has two small branches in neighbouring towns. Abraham & Fothergil offer all the usual legal professional services, but specialise in matrimonial cases and licensing and are also agents for two well-known insurance companies, offering a comprehensive range of insurance policies. William Abraham formed the partnership with James Fothergil in 1948 and, on Mr Fothergil's death in April 1986, he assumed overall responsibility for the firm. Mr Abraham is the Under Sheriff for Winton and a Commissioner for Oaths.

The Winton Office employs 32 people (as shown in the organisation chart on page 66) some of whom work on a part-time basis. Karen Simpkins works mornings only, sharing her job with Katrina Passingham who works in the afternoons and they both work for Kenneth Winters who has been with the firm for 25 years. The job sharing position of Karen and Katrina obviously requires a clear understanding of each other's involvement in his work. Mr Winters heads up a team of solicitors and legal executives dealing with matrimonial and child care cases. Mr Winters is well known in sporting circles as Chairman of Winton Cricket Club, Committee Member of the City Golf Club and President of the County's Badminton Association. In addition, he is Secretary of the Winton Branch of Christian Aid.

SECRETARIAL SERVICES

All partners, solicitors and legal executives have their own secretaries. The firm has considered centralising secretarial services but in view of the need for secretaries to be closely associated with clients, it was decided to retain the 'one-to-one' arrangement. When facing an exceptionally heavy work load a secretary can call upon the services of the secretarial support unit which employs two secretaries to provide back up assistance when required. Mr Porter, the Chief Cashier, has responsibility for the receptionist and telephone services, and ordering and controlling office supplies, including the running of the office copiers which are in great demand by secretaries. All secretaries use electronic typewriters and have access to a word processor. Mr Porter is currently reviewing the word processing needs of secretaries, as he feels that more use could be made of word processors.

The principal means of communication with clients and other firms are letter, telephone and face-to-face. A local delivery 'clearing' system operates between all of the city's solicitors and letters are delivered each evening to a central collecting point at the City Hall. Collections are made each morning, ensuring prompt and reliable transmission of local mail.

LEGAL SECRETARIAL WORK

In addition to the usual range of secretarial duties, Karen has certain tasks which she considers special to her job as secretary to a solicitor, for example:

1 Organising her employer's diary of court cases. As Mr Winter handles a large volume of cases, Karen is required to bring to his attention those which are urgent and require action to be taken;
2 Communicating with clients on the telephone and when they call at the office;
3 Occasionally attending court to sit behind counsel to supply information required from files and make brief notes for Mr Winters.

The legal secretary's work also differs from other secretarial positions in the multiplicity of documents and the manner in which they are typed. For example, these are some of the documents commonly used:

Companies
Certificate of Incorporation of a Company; Contract; Deed of Partnership; Memorandum of Association; Request for Company Search.

Conveyancing
Abstract of Title; Assignment; Completion Statement; Contract of Sale; Conveyance; Declaration of Trust; Deed of Covenant; Lease; Power of Attorney; Request for Search; Transfer.

Litigation
Affidavit; Application for Legal Aid; Particulars of Claim; Statement of Claim.

Matrimonial/Child Care
Certificate for Lodgment; Consent Order; Petition; Statement of Arrangements for Children; Fee Exemption Form; Reconciliation Form; Acknowledgement of Service; Special Procedure Affidavit; Decree Nisi to be made Absolute.

Probate
Estate Account; Will.

General
Agreement; Briefs and Instructions to Counsel.

When the content of a legal document is agreed by the solicitor acting for the other party and typed in final form it is known as an *engrossment*. It is essential that legal documents are typed accurately and without alterations. Punctuation marks are not normally used in legal documents such as agreements, conveyances and wills, but at Abraham & Fothergil they prefer litigation documents such as briefs to counsel and particulars of claim to be fully punctuated. A specimen page of an affidavit typed by Karen is illustrated on page 67.

Client Care

Clients involved in matrimonial and child care cases are often emotionally upset and when they telephone or call in to the office they appreciate a sympathetic ear and an opportunity to talk to someone. In these circumstances the secretary can help by just listening, but using tact and discretion in her response to the client. Without committing her employer to any course of action, Karen may agree to bring any relevant matters to Mr Winters' attention or, if necessary, make an appointment for him to see the client. It is not always easy for Karen to give time to visiting clients as many other equally important and conflicting demands are made on her. For example, on the morning of 1 February she had received dictation for ten letters with accompanying documents from Mr Winters before he left for court; an irate client, Mrs Barkwell, called in to the office to ask Mr Winters why no apparent progress was being made with her case; Mr Abraham's Secretary called on the intercom to agree a date for an urgent partners' meeting; a reporter from the *Advertiser* telephoned to ask if there was any substance in a remark in one of the national daily newspapers that the Captain of Winton Cricket Club was going to be sacked; the Secretary of the City Golf Club telephoned, asking if Mr Winters could attend a special meeting on 8 February; there followed an emotional and desperate telephone call from a client, Robin Parker, demanding to speak to Mr Winters. Robin Parker's wife had left home taking their 6 month old baby girl with her and she had left a note saying that she was leaving him for good. Mr Parker was at his wits end and exclaimed that there was now nothing left to live for! On top of all this, Mr Winters telephoned from court (about 2 miles away) asking Karen to take him a file which he required urgently for a case later that morning.

Staff Deficiencies

Tony Simpkins, one of the secretaries in the Secretarial Support Unit, was allocated to Karen during an exceptionally busy period but unfortunately he appeared to be bored with the work she gave him to do and his 'assistance' created further problems for her. For example, he sent an incorrect set of documents to a solicitor and Karen did not discover the error until she received a phone call from them. She apologised to the firm and sent them the correct documents. Also, after Tony had gone home Karen checked through some documents he had typed and found they were all wrongly dated. Since she did not want to delay the despatch of the documents, she corrected them herself.

One of Mr Winters' clients, Mrs Bramble, sent a letter complaining about Tony's arrogant and abrupt manner on the telephone. She said it gave a very poor impression of the firm to clients. Karen realised that Tony's telephone manner was not as good as it should be, but attributed it to the heavy volume of calls he had to handle. She apologised to Mrs Bramble and explained that Tony was under severe pressure at the time. In view of the problems created by Tony's telephone manner Mr Porter decided to ask Jane Rawlings (a very efficient telephonist) to demonstrate good telephone techniques so that he could make a video to show to Tony and other inexperienced staff.

STAFFING

Mr Madison has responsibility for staffing matters, ie making appointments for new office staff and reviewing the salary levels of existing staff. He is at present considering making a proposal at a partners' meeting to appoint a personnel manager to relieve him of these staffing duties.

Staff meetings are held every quarter on a departmental basis to discuss office procedures and new developments, such as the introduction of word processing, and to provide a means of communicating information to staff. Abraham & Fothergil has managed to retain its 'family firm' atmosphere and image with excellent rapport between all levels of staff and the employees agree that it is a pleasant and friendly environment in which to work.

Abraham & Fothergil, Solicitors

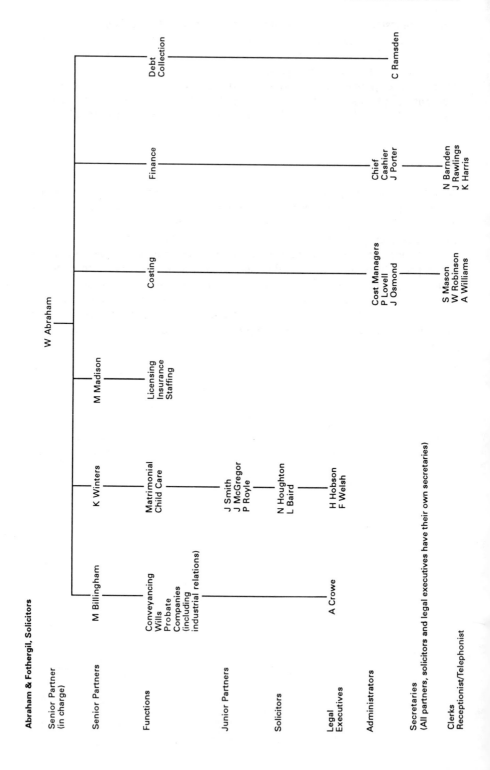

IN THE WINTON COUNTY COURT   No. of Matter: 88 D 099

B E T W E E N:

JUNE MARY JONES   Petitioner

and

BARRY JOHN JONES   Respondent

and

TRACY LYNNE SOUTH   Co-Respondent

A F F I D A V I T

I, JUNE MARY JONES of 15 Ashurst Drive, Trumpton in the County of Winton, Petitioner in the above cause, MAKE OATH and say as follows:

1   I make this Affidavit in support of my Application for financial provision in favour of myself and the children of the family, Peter David Jones born 5th February 1980 and Sarah Jane Jones born 16th May 1982.

2   I was lawfully married to the Respondent on the 28th day of May 1975 and we separated during the month of August 1983.

3   By Separation Agreement dated the 1st day of April 1984 it was agreed that the Respondent would pay to me maintenance at the rate of £277.00 per month together with £130.00 per month to each of the children of the family. In January 1987 the allowance in favour of myself was increased to £312.00 per month. In addition to the maintenance referred to above I receive Child Benefit and Single Parent Allowance amounting to £19.20 per week.

AND NOW FOR YOUR OPINIONS

SECRETARIAL PROCEDURES

8.1 Karen Simpkins' work is of a highly confidential nature. What steps should be taken to preserve this confidentiality? A relative of Joan Hill (Secretary in the Conveyancing Department) is involved in one of Mr Winters' cases. Joan asks Karen to tell her about the case. How should she handle this?

8.2 Why do you think Mr Porter is of the opinion that more use could be made of word processors? How do you envisage word processors being used in a firm of solicitors? What factors should be considered when selecting the word processors?

8.3 Explain how you would devise a reliable system for drawing Mr Winters' attention to cases which are urgent and require action to be taken.

8.4 In addition to the mail received in connection with his work at the firm, Mr Winters receives a great deal of correspondence relating to the cricket club, the golf club, the badminton association and Christian Aid. How would you suggest organising the correspondence for his outside interests so that it is kept apart from his case work? In what ways can the secretary be of assistance to Mr Winters in these outside interests?

STRUCTURE OF BUSINESS

8.5 A client decides to set up his own business building yachts. Describe the insurance policies which Abraham & Fothergil could offer him.

8.6 What advantages would the client gain if he operated as a sole trader and what benefits could he derive by going into partnership with others?

8.7 What contributions does the insurance industry make to:

(a) the economy of the client's business; and
(b) the economy of the country?

8.8 Solicitors in Winton operate a local clearing system. Explain how and why the banks operate a national clearing system.

SECRETARIAL ADMINISTRATION

8.9 The sharing of jobs is becoming increasingly popular. What are the advantages and disadvantages of sharing a senior private secretarial position? How would you suggest Karen and Katrina should establish a clear understanding of each other's involvement in Mr Winters' work?

8.10 How should Karen deal with each of the demands made on her on the morning of 1 February?

8.11 How would you suggest the secretarial services at Abraham & Fothergil's should be co-ordinated and organised, having regard to standardisation of work, supervision, training and staff development?

8.12 Discuss Karen's methods of dealing with Tony Simpkins' incompetence. What action should be taken to prevent a recurrence of these incidents?

MANAGEMENT APPRECIATION

8.13 Mr Madison is considering the appointment of a specialist personnel manager. What role and functions should the personnel manager perform?

8.14 Why do you think Tony Simpkins was bored and lacked motivation? What steps can be taken to encourage Tony to overcome his difficulties?

8.15 What legal aspects of industrial relations could be brought to the attention of Mr Billingham when dealing with company clients?

8.16 Abraham & Fothergil has retained its 'family firm' image. What are the advantages and disadvantages of the family business? Discuss Mr Abraham's role in maintaining this image and say whether the firm's planned developments will have any effect on the way in which the firm is run.

ADDITIONAL STUDENT LEARNING ACTIVITIES

FIND OUT

what Mr Abraham might be required to do as Under Sheriff and a Commissioner for Oaths.

ROLE PLAY

Mr Porter's video recording of Jane Rawlings (Receptionist/telephonist) handling incoming telephone calls.

Barratts – the house builders

COMPANY BACKGROUND

Barratt Developments plc, with its Head Office at Newcastle-upon-Tyne, is the parent company of some nineteen operating companies in different parts of the United Kingdom and the United States, building about 10 000 homes a year. The business was started 27 years ago by the present Chairman, Sir Lawrie Barratt, who has also undertaken extensive building projects in the USA, capturing a substantial portion of the American house-building market.

Partnership projects

Over half of Barratt's current production in the UK is in the inner cities and urban areas where they are working on numerous joint ventures with local authorities, central government, housing associations and building societies. In these partnership projects Barratts are providing a mix of homes for rent, shared ownership, sale at low cost to local authority nominees and open sale. For example, a Liverpool Docklands Conversion Scheme created 114 modern homes in a disused Victorian Warehouse at Wapping Dock as a result of a major urban renewal project by Barratts in partnership with the Merseyside Development Corporation, the Merseyside Improved Housing Association and several leading building societies. Similar projects are in varying stages of development at Edinburgh, Glasgow, Rhondda, Poole, Newcastle-upon-Tyne, Bradford, Leeds, Nottingham, Peterborough and London.

Brighton's Marina Village

At the time of writing this case study, Barratts were completing the first of their luxury waterside townhouses at the Brighton Marina Village. Set behind remote-controlled electronic gates on the first promontory and near the village square, these luxury properties offer four and five bedroom accommodation. Strategically-placed balconies, terraces and magnificent bay windows allow residents panoramic views of the inner lagoons. Each house also has its own private mooring.

Brent Walker, in co-operation with Barratts, are creating a leisure complex which will include a sports centre, an international four-star hotel, night club, multi-screen cinema, health hydro and an indoor water theme park. As well as Brent Walker's own restaurant and cocktail bar, designed to reflect traditional Venetian architecture, the village square will have a wide variety of public houses, cafes, bistros, restaurants, boutiques and other speciality shops.

House exchange plan

Barratt's offers a house exchange plan which allows customers to exchange their old house for a new Barratt house, with obvious advantages to both parties.

CASE STUDY ORGANISATION

Hazel Churcher, the secretary portrayed in this case study, works for the Managing Director and the Finance Director of Barratt Southampton Limited which was established six years ago in a modern office block at Eastleigh. Hazel Churcher had previously been a secretary in the company's sales department before taking on the more senior position, filling a vacancy caused by the previous secretary leaving to have a baby. Fortunately Hazel was able to learn a great deal about the job from her before she left. She enjoys the added responsibility, the chance to use her initiative and her greater involvement in the work of the company.

At the Eastleigh Head Office 30 staff are employed, and a further 60 staff (site managers, quantity surveyors, etc) at the various construction sites around the south coast. The organisation chart on page 74 shows the staff employed at the Head Office of Barratt Southampton Limited.

Personnel matters

Each head of department in the company has responsibility for the welfare and supervision of their own employees, although the Finance Director administers the recruitment, selection, employment and training of office staff.

SECRETARY'S CONTACTS

Hazel's position in the company brings her into contact with many different people, as indicated in the chart on page 72.

Hazel's involvement with these contacts:

Managing Director   She provides the usual range of secretarial services for the two directors, the MD's work normally taking precedence. Travel arrangements are normally made from the parent company's head office but Hazel is involved in verifying train times and purchasing tickets. She services meetings, ie organises catering facilities, arranges dates and notifies participants, takes the minutes and types the draft copies for approval. Hazel has experienced some difficulty in taking the minutes at meetings because of the technical nature of the discussions.

Finance Director

She provides secretarial services as indicated above and processes papers for insurance claims.

Board of Directors

Communications with the Managing Director and Finance Director. Prepares papers for board meetings.

Head Office Staff

Communications with the Managing Director and Finance Director. A social committee has recently been formed to organise social events for the staff such as a river boat shuffle, a day at the races and a Christmas dinner dance. Hazel is a member of this committee and she organises the dinner dance.

Secretarial and Clerical Staff

As the senior secretary Hazel is responsible for supervising all of the secretarial and clerical staff at the Eastleigh Office. She interviews new staff and organises cover for secretarial staff when they are absent, re-allocating work as necessary.

Work Experience Pupils and YTS Trainees

Hazel deals with correspondence concerning the attachment of work experience pupils from local schools and the employment of YTS trainees, preparing their work programmes and supervising them.

Customers

Communications with the Managing Director and Finance Director.

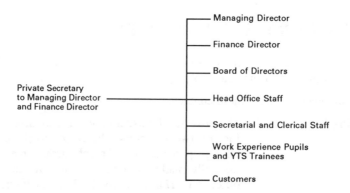

There are occasions when Hazel has to work overtime in order to cope with the intense pressure of business, especially when preparing papers for a board meeting or for a special project. Consideration will be given to the employment of a junior secretary to assist Hazel. It is, however, difficult for someone new to the work to know which of Mr Russell's telephone calls should be put through to him, which should be redirected to others, or which dealt with by the secretary. It requires tact and diplomacy to redirect callers to another director or manager when the person called is engaged with other business. The calls are from various sources, for example on the morning of 1 March Hazel received the following calls:

1 Mr Purkiss, who had 15 acres of land for sale and wanted to know whether the Company was interested in buying it.
2 Jane Potts, a salesperson for kitchen units.
3 John Jackson, an employee working on one of the sites, who wished to raise a matter concerning his working conditions.
4 Mr T Hartley, the Chairman of the Board.
5 Mrs B Carter, requesting a donation from the company for Oxfam.
6 Mr Russell's wife.
7 Sir Lawrie Barratt, Chairman of the Parent Company.
8 Mr T Brown, Head of Business Studies at the local College of Further Education, requesting a work experience placement with the company.

Company accounts

The following figures were extracted from the company's accounts for the two years prior to the date when the case study was prepared:

	1987	1988
	£000	*£000*
Fixed assets	94	93
Current assets	19 963	22 962
Long-term liabilities (Creditors due after more than one year)	2 789	–
Current liabilities (Creditors due within one year)	13 885	7 699
Capital and reserves (including 500 000 ordinary shares of £1 each authorised and issued)	3 383	7 556
Turnover	13 890	40 471
Net profit/(loss) before taxation	(216)	6 600
Tax on profit/(loss)	(67)	2 316
Net profit/(loss) after taxation	(149)	4 284

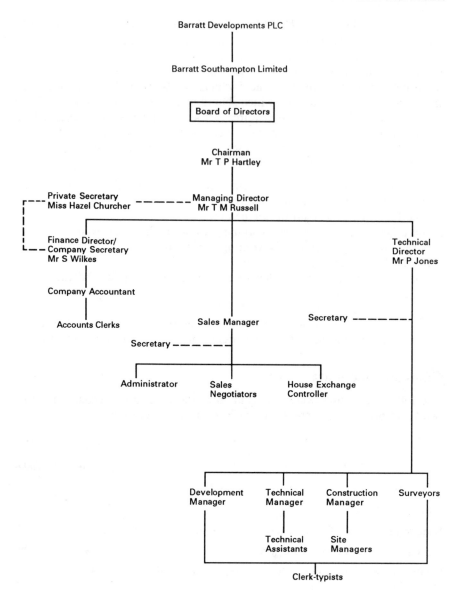

AND NOW FOR YOUR VIEWS

SECRETARIAL PROCEDURES

9.1 An interview for a new junior secretary has to be arranged and conducted during Hazel's absence on holiday. Prepare a checklist of action to be taken: (*a*) before the interview; (*b*) at the interview and (*c*) after the interview.

9.2 Explain how you would deal with each of the telephone calls received for Mr Russell on the morning of 1 March.

9.3 Hazel's predecessor left Barratt to have a baby. What maternity provisions concerning pay and leave were available to her and what action must she take in order to qualify for such provisions?

9.4 Hazel enjoyed the added responsibility given to her to use her initiative. In what ways do you think she could do this and how would the directors benefit from her initiative?

STRUCTURE OF BUSINESS

9.5 Why do you think Barratt has entered into joint ventures with local and central government authorities for the building of homes? In what other ways have public authorities had an influence on business?

9.6 Barratt is seeking to develop trade in the USA. How can the UK improve its trade with overseas countries? Why is such trade important to the economy of a country?

9.7 What are the 'obvious advantages to both parties' of the Barratt House Exchange Plan? Are there any disadvantages?

9.8 Discuss the effects an increase in the bank lending rate is likely to have on the demand for new houses.

SECRETARIAL ADMINISTRATION

9.9 Hazel's position brought her into contact with seven different categories of people. How would you expect her relationship to differ with each of these people?

9.10 How would you solve the problem of taking minutes of meetings when the discussion involves technical matters? What advice on taking minutes of meetings would you give to a secretary deputising for you?

9.11 Draw up a checklist for organising the Christmas dinner dance. Indicate when each action would have to be initiated and enclose copies of all relevant correspondence sent in connection with these arrangements.

9.12 What information would you expect Hazel to obtain from her predecessor when she prepared herself to take over the position of secretary to the Managing Director and Finance Director? In what other ways should she prepare for her new position?

MANAGEMENT APPRECIATION

9.13 Comment on the significance of the figures extracted from the company accounts for the two years and state the return on capital employed and the ratios for net profit and working capital.

9.14 Hazel has responsibility for re-allocating work for the secretarial staff when staff are absent. What should she do if a member of staff was persistently absent for trivial reasons and the staff who were asked to cover for her resented having to do the extra work?

9.15 Mr Wilkes has asked Hazel to draw up a job description and specification for a new junior secretary to assist her in her work. What should they contain and how will they assist in the recruitment and selection of the new employee?

9.16 What information does the organisation chart in this case study give you? Mr Wilkes is in a line relationship with Mr Russell. What does this mean? What is Hazel's relationship to Mr Russell and how does this differ from that of Mr Wilkes?

ADDITIONAL STUDENT LEARNING ACTIVITIES

FIND OUT

what information Hazel could locate in the following books kept in the Managing Director's office:

Directory of Directors
The City Directory
Housing Year Book
Directory of Official Architecture & Planning

ROLE PLAY

the telephone callers and the secretary handling them on the morning of 1 March – record your conversations and discuss the results with your colleagues.

A local branch of the Midland Bank

This case study is based on the work of Ann Chambers, the secretary in a small branch of the Midland Bank.

A small town branch of the Midland Bank.

HISTORICAL BACKGROUND

The Midland Bank was founded in Birmingham in 1836 by Charles Geach, when it was known as the Birmingham and Midland Bank. Throughout the remainder of the 19th century and up to 1918 considerable developments and expansion took place with mergers, amalgamations and the setting up of new branches in England and Wales. Throughout this century Midland has featured as one of the 'Big Four' clearing banks in the UK and, since the 1950s, its interests have become highly diversified. The modern Midland Group includes Forward Trust (acquired in 1958), the merchant bank Samuel Montagu & Co Limited (wholly owned since 1973) and the Thomas Cook Travel Group (acquired in 1972). In recent years Midland has also developed interests abroad with the establishment of an international network of subsidiary and associated companies.

COMPANY ORGANISATION

Today the Midland Bank Group has a nationwide UK network of over 3000 offices and branches. The head office in London has the following sectors:

Group Finance
Group Personnel
Information Technology
UK Banking
Wholesale Banking (including international and investment)

The divisions and departments which operate within these five sectors include:

General management; Administration department; Agriculture department; Audit and Inspection department; Clearing department; Credit and Risk department – Lending; Economics department; Electronic Banking and Customer Payment Services; Group Corporate Planning department; Group Management Services; Group Treasury; Information Technology department; Marketing department; Midland Personal Financial Services; Midland Stockbrokers; Planning department; Premises department; Public Relations department; Secretary's office; Solicitors and Legal department.

Branch functions

All branches offer the same services and have similar jobs, but no two branches are identical, varying in size both in number of staff and customers. The type of business transacted and the type of customers vary too, depending on whether the branch is situated in a city centre, a suburb, a country town or a small village. Every branch carries out a considerable number of functions, the most important of which are concerned with taking deposits, lending money to individuals and businesses, and transmitting money on a nationwide and worldwide basis. The branch manager is responsible for the smooth and efficient running of the branch and this entails not only maintaining cost-effective systems but ensuring the welfare of staff and a first-class service for customers.

Changes and developments are continually taking place in banking systems, the most far-reaching of which is the branch controller system with its new generation of computer terminals designed to handle the expected growth in business. This system improves both efficiency and quality of work by automating many of the more repetitive tasks. At the time of writing this case study the Midland, in co-operation with the National Westminster Bank and the Royal Bank of Scotland were planning a new initiative with EFTPOS (electronic funds transfer at point of sale) which is to be called *Switch*. This new service will allow Switch cardholders to pay for goods and services without the need to write cheques or use cash. They will be able to pay electronically at any retail establishment displaying the Switch logo by handing the card to the sales assistant, who will pass the card through a point-of-sale device. A receipt will be automatically printed for the cardholder to sign and verify the transaction. Once the signature has been checked the transaction is completed. By this means the cardholders will have a faster, more efficient way to pay and they will be debited within the cheque clearing timescale of three days.

CASE STUDY SITUATION

Ann Chambers is Secretary to Mr Philip Cox, the Manager at a small town branch which employs 11 staff (*see* the branch organisation chart given on page 82). The equipment at the branch office consists of an electronic typewriter, a text processor, an audio transcriber, an office copier and a computer terminal linked to the bank's computer centre in London.

Ann is responsible for the following duties:

- Typing the Manager's correspondence
  - letters to customers and Area Office (*see* the specimen form letter on page 83 confirming an overdraft facility)
  - notes on customers' accounts
  - reports to Area Office
  - general correspondence
- Typing the Senior Clerk's correspondence
  - as above
- Preparing 'personalised' standard letters, as required by the Manager and Senior Clerk
  - these are used for reminding customers when their accounts are overdrawn above their permitted limits, revising a customer's overdraft limit, requesting a bank reference, etc.

- General office typing
- Keeping the Office Diary and making appointments for:
  - the Manager
  - the Senior Clerk
  - the personal financial services representative
  - customers for wills to be arranged, financial advice given, etc.

- Telephone enquiries
- Filing
- Amending and updating the   – a printed directory giving names
  branch directory   of personnel and telephone
                                            numbers for all branches, area
                                            offices and head office
                                            departments
- Making travel arrangements   – this usually involves hiring a car
- Providing staff relief (mostly at
  lunch times) for the enquiry
  counter and as cashier
- Promoting and marketing the   – involving telephone calls, callers at
  bank's products and services   the enquiry desk and training
                                            school pupils to look after their
                                            'mock' bank branches

There are times when Ann sometimes has to work under considerable pressure, switching from one job to another, in order to deal with the pressing needs of the branch. For example, during a typical week in August, in addition to her usual full in-tray of typing tasks, she could have been required to deal with any of the following hypothetical situations:

1 The Senior Operations Manager of the Area Office telephoned to speak to Mr Cox who had not returned to the bank from a business luncheon appointment.

2 A customer called at the bank (without an appointment) to see Mr Cox.

3 The Manager was required to attend an important meeting at Area Office and his car would not start. Very few staff members had cars at the branch or could be spared from their duties to drive him to the meeting.

4 Ann often gets involved in sales activities which she enjoys. A customer is referred to her by a cashier during a busy lunch time period when the Manager and other senior members of the staff are already engaged or at lunch. The gentleman pays a cheque for £5000 into his current account with an instruction to transfer these funds to a building society investment account.

The branch has a YTS trainee on its staff and also assists in providing work experience for local school pupils.

OFFICE SERVICES

Regular staff/management meetings are held as a means of disseminating branch information and office procedures. A monthly newsheet issued throughout the bank group keeps staff in touch with new developments, new services and systems, staffing matters (promotions, appointments, retirements, etc.) and social activities.

One of the clerks in the branch has responsibility for requisitioning and controlling stationery supplies which are ordered from a central warehouse. Incoming mail is sorted and distributed by the Senior Clerk and Secretary and outgoing mail is handled in rotation by the clerical staff. Mail is franked and Post Office bags (red for 1st class mail and green for 2nd class mail) are used to deliver the post to the post office. Mail for the Area Office is collected daily by a messenger van.

Every member of staff is expected to comply with a strict code of practice for security as the confidentiality of customers' records and the security of the premises is of prime importance.

Staffing

The recruitment, selection and employment of staff at branches is organised by the Area Office. Annual staff appraisal reports are made by the Manager for the Area Office and promotion is based on performance, in competition with similarly graded staff in the bank. In-house training occurs at branch and area levels as well as at the Bank's Training Centres. Staff are encouraged to study for the Chartered Institute of Bankers examinations and successful completion of these examinations is an important aspect of a banking employee's career development. Leave may be granted for employees to study for such examinations.

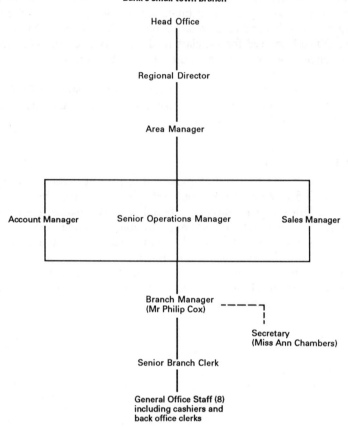

Bank's small town branch

Head Office

Regional Director

Area Manager

Account Manager   Senior Operations Manager   Sales Manager

Branch Manager
(Mr Philip Cox)

Secretary
(Miss Ann Chambers)

Senior Branch Clerk

General Office Staff (8)
including cashiers and
back office clerks

Midland Bank
Confirmation of Overdraft Facility
for Personal Customers

Name _____ Current Account No _____

I am pleased to confirm the facility agreed with you today, the details of which are set out below.

TYPE OF FACILITY	CheckOver/Overdraft
LIMIT	£_____
INTEREST RATE TO BE CHARGED	CheckOver Rate, presently_____% per month

APR_____%

OR

_____% over Midland Base Rate, presently_____% per annum

APR_____%

ARRANGEMENT FEE	£_____
EXPIRY DATE	The last day of_____ 19_____

The Terms and Conditions relating to this facility are shown overleaf. If you wish to vary, extend or exceed these arrangements, please contact us.

DATE_____ SIGNATURE_____

BRANCH_____ TITLE_____

Stock No 2221-0

The Listening Bank

QUESTIONS FOR YOUR CONSIDERATION

SECRETARIAL PROCEDURES

10.1 (*a*) Draft a standard letter from the Manager to customers drawing attention to their overdrawn current accounts. Leave blanks for the variable information.

(*b*) What equipment would you use to prepare the standard letters and to insert the variable information?

10.2 What effect will the increased use of EFTPOS have on the office procedures of a retail business and the bank?

10.3 Explain how you would expect Ann to deal with each of the situations which occurred during the week in August.

10.4 A new Senior Branch Clerk has recently been appointed to the branch and she has had no previous experience of dictating for audio-transcription. You are asked to write some simple instructions (which do not include the operation of the equipment) to guide her in recording dictation so that you can transcribe her work quickly and efficiently.

STRUCTURE OF BUSINESS

10.5 In what ways can a commercial bank help a person who is about to set up in business for the first time?

10.6 How does the Bank of England control the activities of the Midland Bank?

10.7 The Midland Bank employs stockbrokers at its Head Office. Describe the work of the Stock Exchange and the role of stockbrokers in it.

10.8 A business which needs to increase its capital can obtain it in various ways from a commercial bank. Suggest three possible bank services that could be used and discuss the merits and drawbacks of each. What other sources could be used to acquire capital?

SECRETARIAL ADMINISTRATION

10.9 Meetings can be very time-consuming and sometimes unproductive. How can the Chairman of the Staff/Management Meetings ensure that they are cost effective and productive?

10.10 The secretaries in a busy branch of the bank have to be both versatile, ie capable of secretarial duties as well as helping out with counter duties, and effective in time management to deal with the many demands made upon them. Explain three methods which you might use to ensure that work is dealt with efficiently and on time.

10.11 Why do you think the bank attaches great importance to its public relations? How can Ann enhance the Bank's public relations when she is engaged in promoting and marketing the Bank's products and services?

10.12 Mr Cox has agreed to act as Chairman at a Chamber of Commerce Annual Dinner to be held in the nearby County Hall. There will be two guest speakers, one a member of the peerage, neither of whom Mr Cox has met. Outline the arrangements his secretary should make for him.

MANAGEMENT APPRECIATION

10.13 Suggest how costs can be reduced and cost-effectiveness increased in the administration of a bank.

10.14 'A bank with a happy and competent staff is more likely to have satisfied customers'. How would you expect the Manager to achieve these ideals?

10.15 Discuss the impact of new technology on the role of the Manager of a Bank Branch.

10.16 What are the advantages and disadvantages of separating the functions of recruitment, selection and employment of staff from the work base, as in the case of the bank where these tasks are centralised at the Area Office?

ADDITIONAL STUDENT LEARNING ACTIVITIES

FIND OUT

what personal services the bank can offer you and what effect the Financial Services Act has had on these services.

ROLE PLAY

Ann's talk to a small group of school pupils visiting the branch who have asked her to tell them about her work as a bank secretary and what is expected from young people joining the bank.

Warner-Lambert (UK) Limited

THE INTERNATIONAL ORGANISATION

When William R Warner began his pharmacy business in Philadelphia in 1856 he laid the foundations of the Warner-Lambert Company, which was to become one of the world's leading health care companies generating over £2 billion in annual sales and employing more than 33 000 people in 140 countries. The business now manufactures a wide range of products: ethical pharmaceuticals, pharmacy medicines, medicated confectionery, toiletries, veterinary and pet care products. The following sales financial data relating to two recent years of trading indicates the magnitude of Warner-Lambert's International marketing operations:

Sales financial data

(in millions of US$)

Year	Ethical products	Non-prescription products	Gums and mints	Other products	Total
19(1)					
Net Sales	964	1077	678	384	3103
Cost of goods sold					1053
19(2)					
Net Sales	1093	1195	777	420	3485
Cost of goods sold					1170

The United Kingdom development and operations

Warner-Lambert (UK) Limited is one of the largest operations in the international network of the company and also the headquarters for a region covering Britain, Ireland and Scandinavia. The company came to Britain in 1932 when British affiliates of Warner, Hudnut and Lambert were registered in London and in 1956 a plant was opened at Eastleigh in Hampshire. The acquisition of the Parke-Davis Company in 1970 strengthened Warner-

Lambert's British business, since Parke-Davis had been well known since the turn of the century.

The Eastleigh factory manufactured toiletry and hair care products as well as many pharmaceuticals. The Head Office for the Region was also located at the Eastleigh factory complex but, because of the expansion of its operations, it was not long before accommodation was in short supply and some of its departments had to be housed in rented accommodation in other parts of the town. Well over half of Warner-Lambert's UK production is for export, which is administered from Eastleigh, where there is an export warehouse and shipping department. These provide the essential links between production and the company's export customers by co-ordinating sales forecasts, servicing the customers' orders and the associated complex documentation as well as shipping the products. In some instances, notably Europe and North America, the products are supplied to other Warner-Lambert affiliates who arrange their distribution and sales in the countries for which they are responsible. In all other areas, particularly the Middle East, sales are made direct to distributors. The marketing and sales operation for nineteen African countries is co-ordinated from Eastleigh, where marketing and technical support, advertising material, sales training and information is supplied to the local sales forces.

A new factory was opened in Pontypool, South Wales in 1971 to manufacture the bulk of the company's pharmaceutical, pharmacy medicines and toiletries. In 1987 all production activities at Eastleigh were moved to Pontypool to enhance economies of scale and to make manufacturing more efficient. As a result of rationalisation of work and an examination of manning levels some redundancies were unavoidable and these included clerks, secretaries and managers. These and other employees who decided not to move to Pontypool or could not be relocated to other jobs were given re-training courses and a job shop was installed on the Eastleigh premises. The announcement of the closure was made 18 months in advance.

As a result of the move, the Eastleigh site was sold for redevelopment, but as it was decided to leave the Regional Head Office at Eastleigh, a new modern office block large enough to accommodate all departments was leased from the new owners. At the time when this case study was written the company was making final arrangements to move into the new building. Arrangements were also being made for the Chairman of the parent company to visit Eastleigh to see the new headquarters.

CASE STUDY SITUATION

Lyn Applin has been with the company five years, gaining experience in the Human Resources and Regional Communications Departments before taking up her present position 18 months ago as Secretary/Administrator to Mr A W Yates, the Regional Finance Director. Lyn is responsible for a Clerk-Typist/ Word Processor Operator who assists her with the work of the Finance Division. Lyn's job consists of:

1 Day-to-day running of the Finance Division's secretarial/administrative function.
2 Providing a para-legal service, undertaking various assigned tasks associated with the company's secretarial functions.
3 Effecting the renewal of insurance premiums, maintenance of records and routine insurance claims.
4 Supervising the Finance Division's Clerk-Typist/WP Operator.
5 Providing a highly confidential secretarial service to the Regional Finance Director, UK Finance Controller/Company Secretary and Regional Development/Acquisitions Manager.

The person profile

The person profile (personnel specification) for Lyn's position identifies the following:

Special aptitudes and skills

- High degree of accuracy and speed in preparing correspondence and legal documentation
- Good organisational and administrative skills
- Ability to delegate to and supervise other secretarial resources ensuring high level of service is given
- Ability to work under pressure and to assign work priorities
- Ability to act on own initiative in dealing with routine mail and correspondence and dealing with internal/external queries
- Ability to deal with people with tact and diplomacy, anticipate problems and stay calm in crises
- Thorough knowledge of regional organisation
- Basic knowledge of company secretarial practice

Demands

- Required to work under pressure with constantly changing priorities and to work overtime as the need arises
- Ability to think fast and respond to all demands with tact and diplomacy
- Ability to co-ordinate and carry out procedures on decisions made regarding the administration of the Division

Decisions taken

- Assignment and priority of work of Clerk-Typist/WP Operator
- Whether to deal with correspondence personally or refer to management
- In absence of Finance Director ensure urgent matters are dealt with personally or by appropriate Manager
- Re-allocating and assigning secretarial work within the Division or from outside source
- All arrangements in respect of meetings

Special features

- The job entails highly confidential work which often accompanies urgency, working under pressure and using discretion
- Deputises for the Secretary to the Regional President, when required

Staff appraisal and annual review

Annual reviews are based on regular performance appraisals. Each member of staff is allocated a certain number of goals to be achieved during the course of a year. For example, Lyn's current goals include:

- Review the present follow-up system
- Reorganise the filing and develop a central integrated system for the Finance Director, Company Secretary, Business Development Manager and Financial Controller
- Prepare documentation for company annual returns and annual general meetings and ensure filing with the Companies Registration Office in due time

Lyn works adjacent to Mr Yates' office in a large open plan office and she has a stand-alone word processor, an electronic typewriter with half-screen and access to a copier, telex and fax.

Meetings and conferences

Lyn recently organised a Planning Review Conference at a London hotel which staff from all parts of the world attended. She organises regular communications meetings for the staff of the Regional Finance Division and regional board meetings. Lyn finds it useful to use a meetings control sheet (*see* page 94) as a check list of action to be taken.

Work priorities

At the beginning of each day Lyn lists the jobs in her 'in-tray' under the following headings:

A Urgent – must be done today – top priority
B Not so urgent – but important
C Not urgent – less important – low priority

She completes category **A** first and then proceeds with **B** and if time permits **C**. Lyn had an interesting experience when she attended an external course with her boss on Time Management. She learnt from this course that when she has top priority work to do she should be more assertive in preventing those who may wish to divert her attention from the job in hand.

Lyn does the filing herself and always tries to do it every day to keep the office clear of papers and to ensure that the files are always up to date. She hopes to pass this task on to her assistant when she has acquired sufficient knowledge of the Division's work. The files at present are arranged by subject classification in vertical filing cabinets, but in the new office block

Lyn Applin at a Finance Division Management Meeting chaired by Mr A W Yates, Regional Finance Director (on Lyn's right), where she takes the minutes.

Lyn will use new lateral filing cabinets. A bring forward file is used for following up correspondence.

When Lyn took over her present post she acquired an office packed full of files and papers and the first task Mr Yates asked her to do was to remove as much paperwork as possible from the office. She set up a new filing system, removing the files not requiring Mr Yates's attention and disposing of files duplicating records kept elsewhere.

Travel arrangements

Lyn's work in connection with travel arrangements involves:

- preparing itineraries (see specimen on page 93)
- arranging cars for short journeys or to/from the airport
- booking hotels
- purchasing tickets from the travel agency
- arranging for travellers cheques/currency to be supplied
- checking medical requirements
- making application for visa and passport renewal (if required)

Office services

There is a central mail room where incoming and outgoing mail are processed.

The mail room clerk delivers the mail to the divisions in the morning and collects outgoing mail for the post at 0900, 1100, 1415 and 1515. After 1515 the divisions are responsible for stamping and posting their own mail, using postage stamps if urgent. Each division orders its own stationery requirements. Lyn's assistant is responsible for ordering and storing stationery in the Finance Division.

Lyn has responsibility for keeping a checklist of staff present in the Finance Division which she has to produce if the premises are vacated for a fire or some other emergency.

STAFF RELATIONS AND EMPLOYMENT

The selection and employment of staff is normally undertaken by the Personnel Department, but occasionally the senior secretaries assist. Lyn was involved in the appointment of her assistant who took the place of a temporary typist. The temporary typist had done the job for some time and expected to be offered the post and was bitterly disappointed when Lyn had the difficult task of telling her that she had not been appointed. At the present time the company has discontinued the practice of employing 'temps' which created a problem for Lyn in re-allocating secretarial support services when two vacancies occurred and there was no-one to fill them. The Export Manager's Secretary left and the vacancy was filled by an existing member of staff; however before she took up the position she obtained another post within the company, leaving two unfilled posts.

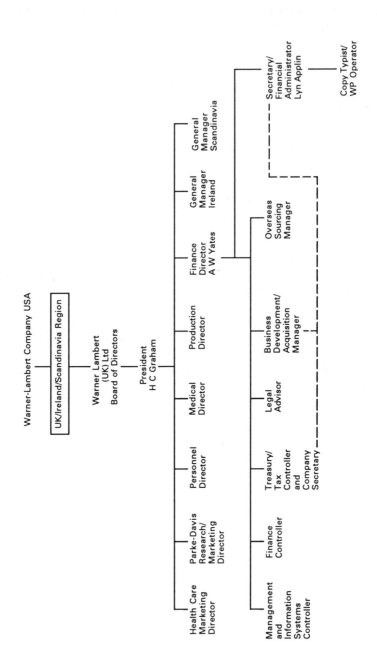

ITINERARY – A W YATES
Week commencing Monday 1st August

Monday 1st

        Office

12.30   Lunch with Warburgs – Table for 4 booked at Crest

18.45   Depart Office

        Dinner – Finance Group & Regional President – Table for 7 booked at Lainstone House 19.00 for 19.30.

Tuesday 2nd

        Office

Wednesday 3rd

07.30   Pick up arranged from home to office

14.50   Transport arranged from Office to London Heathrow

16.00   Flight BA816 departing for Dublin

        Overnight accommodation:

        Fitzpatrick Castle Hotel
        Killiney
        Co. Dublin
        Ireland

        Tel: 0001-851533

Thursday 4th

08.15   Pick up at Killiney Castle

08.30   Warner Lambert (Ireland) Offices
        Tel: 0001-853277

        Overnight:

        Fitzpatrick Castle Hotel

Friday 5th

08.15   Pick up at Killiney Castle

08.30   Pharmaceutical/Gum Base Plant Tour and meetings

17.00   Depart for airport

18.05   Flight BA 817 to London Heathrow

19.10   Flight arrival
        Transport arranged from airport to home.
        Mail to be delivered by driver.

REGIONAL FINANCE DIVISION

MEETINGS CONTROL SHEET   (PAGE 1 OF 2)

SUBJECT _____   STARTING TIME _____

DATE   _____   DURATION APPROX _____

PEOPLE TO CONTACT

EXT/TEL NO	NAME	PROPOSED DATES/TIMES	COMMENT/NOTES

MEETINGS CONTROL SHEET (PAGE 2 OF 2)

REFRESHMENTS   ROOMS
COFFEE _____   OWN OFFICE _____
TEA   _____   BOARDROOM   _____
LUNCH   _____   V.D.R.   _____
                                           LECTURE RM _____
                                           OTHER   _____
                                           OUTSIDE   _____

NOTIFIED: NAME OF CONTACT/NUMBER
_____   _____

PAPERWORK/ACTION   BOOKED: _____
AGENDA COMPLETED _____   CONFIRMED: _____
            SENT OUT _____   SPECIAL REQUIREMENTS:
MINUTES COMPLETED _____   EQUIPMENT: _____
            SENT OUT _____   _____
OTHER ITEMS   _____   REFRESH: _____
                                           PARKING: _____
                                           DETAILS COMPLETED: _____
ANY FOLLOW UP ACTION: RECEPTION/SWITCHBOARD
                                           INFORMED:
_____   _____

ACTION AFTER MEETING:
_____

LPA/OCT.19

WHAT IS YOUR OPINION?

SECRETARIAL PROCEDURES

11.1 (*a*) How would you 'remove as much paperwork as possible from the office' as requested by Mr Yates?
(*b*) What are the advantages of using lateral filing compared with the existing vertical filing?

11.2 Prepare a 'person profile' for the post of Clerk-Typist/WP Operator (Assistant to Lyn) or, if you are employed, for your post.

11.3 The Management and Information Systems Controller has asked you to give him your ideas for a system of centralising the ordering and control of stationery. Write a memo giving your suggestions and say what advantages centralisation would have over the present system.

11.4 How would the procedure and documentation of a board meeting differ from those used by Mr Yates for the Finance Division's Communications meetings?

STRUCTURE OF BUSINESS

11.5 What is contained in the 'complex documentation' associated with the export business? What assistance does the government give to exporters?

11.6 Give reasons why countries participate in international trading. What artificial barriers to such trade may be imposed by central government?

11.7 How can Warner-Lambert justify the expenditure incurred in providing a marketing and sales operation for African countries. What other departments are affected by a decision to increase the marketing function and in what way?

11.8 Lyn is responsible for effecting the renewal of insurance premiums. What risks are the company likely to insure against? What do you understand by insurance premiums, insurance policies and insurable interest?

SECRETARIAL ADMINISTRATION

11.9 You are asked to make the necessary arrangements for the Chairman of the parent company in America to visit Eastleigh in three months' time to see the new head-quarters. He will stay for three days and will be accompanied by his wife. Draw up a checklist of the action to be taken and indicate when each item should be initiated and by whom.

11.10 How would you solve Lyn's problem of maintaining the secretarial support services when the two vacancies occurred and it was not possible to employ 'temps'?

11.11 Suggest how Lyn should decide:

(*a*) 'the assignment and priority of work of the Clerk-Typist/WP Operator'.
and
(*b*) 'Whether to deal with correspondence personally or refer it to management'.

11.12 Devise 'achievement goals' for Lyn's Assistant or, if you are employed, for yourself.

MANAGEMENT APPRECIATION

11.13 What factors would Warner-Lambert take into account when making the decision to move its factory from Eastleigh to Pontypool? Would the separation of production from the other departments of Head Office create any problems?

11.14 What would you expect to learn from a Time Management Course? Is it a good idea for the secretary to be accompanied by her employer on such a course?

11.15 Analyse the sales financial data for the Warner-Lambert Company, and for the two years:

(*a*) state the percentage sales for each product group and illustrate them with pie charts;
(*b*) state the cost of goods sold as a percentage of sales;
(*c*) calculate the percentage change in net sales for year 19(2) compared with 19(1);
(*d*) comment on the sales performance of the company.

11.16 (*a*) What legislation governs the employment of staff?
(*b*) What statutory rights would the employees of Warner-Lambert have had when they were made redundant?

ADDITIONAL STUDENT LEARNING ACTIVITIES

Assuming that Mr Yates is required to visit China on business:

FIND OUT

(a) health requirements (vaccinations etc.)
(b) visa requirement (if one is required, the address where it can be obtained)
(c) time difference in relation to GMT
(d) name of capital and major cities
(e) official language
(f) currency

ROLE PLAY

Lyn's conversation with the temporary typist explaining that she had not been appointed and that her employment with the company would be terminated in a month's time.

University College Hospital and Middlesex School of Medicine

HISTORICAL BACKGROUND

This historical review starts in 1746 when the infirmary in Windmill Street, off Tottenham Court Road, London, changed its name to 'The Middlesex Hospital' and students received permission to 'walk the hospital'. As the Hospital grew and surgeon-pupils were allowed to join physician-pupils, the Medical Society was formed, which has now completed 210 years of distinguished membership.

University College was founded in 1826. The initial aim of the founders was to create a 'University of London'. Among the thirty foundation chairs were seven in medicine. The surgeon, Sir Charles Bell, was the first of the great figures common to the histories of both Schools of Medicine. A close association between the College and The Middlesex seemed inevitable but it was not to be.

In 1831 University College decided to build a hospital and by 1834 it was opened. Students there were Robert Liston, who in 1848 performed the first operation under anaesthetic in Europe and Joseph Lister, who was later to revolutionise surgery through his work on infection and antisepsis.

In 1835 it was advocated that there should be established The Middlesex Hospital Medical School and within six months the Medical School was opened in newly constructed premises. In 1836 University College London (UCL) was founded, while a new corporate body designated as the 'University of London' was created with power to grant degrees to candidates having completed courses at University College, King's College or such other institutions. The Middlesex Hospital Medical School became such an institution in 1900, after amalgamation of the Hospital and School in 1896.

In 1914 Sir John Bland-Sutton, a famous surgeon on the staff, gave the Medical School added prestige by building and endowing the Institute of Pathology, which bears his name. A little earlier, a large bequest had provided a new cancer wing and research laboratories for the study of cancer. The Hospital and School had been identified with research into the causes and treatment of cancer since the formation of the Cancer Charity in 1792 and continues to play an active part.

In 1980 University College Hospital was incorporated into University College London as the Faculty of Clinical Sciences. Thus a School of

Medicine in its entirety was formed at University College which consisted of two Faculties: Medical Sciences and Clinical Sciences. In 1985–86 this merged with the Middlesex Hospital Medical School to form a single School of Medicine within University College London, to be called the University College and Middlesex School of Medicine. This was inaugurated in November 1987 and came into being after a Private Act of Parliament was passed on 1 March 1988.

CASE STUDY

The historical background gives an insight into the complicated merging of two institutions and our case study is concerned with the roles of Medical Secretaries and administrative secretarial duties at the School of Medicine, situated in London. Margaret Garden is Assistant Administrative Secretary at the Faculty of Clinical Sciences and runs the Medical School Office. Within her office there are two secretaries, Sue and Diana, and a junior shorthand-typist, Sejal Patel.

The main areas of responsibility of the Medical School Office are concerned with the medical students who proceed to the Medical School via a two-year pre-clinical course at the Faculty of Medical Sciences and possibly an additional year's course to obtain a BSc. At this point students decide whether to continue on the two and three-quarter years clinical studies which involves ward work, hospital experience and further studies, before proceeding to six months as a House Physician, six months as House Surgeon, obtaining the Certificates of Satisfactory Service, and the approval from the Dean for acceptance by the General Medical Council. The Medical School Office (see page 102) is responsible for the organisation of courses for the students, covering an Introductory Course to Clinical Studies, Pathology Course and Revision Course, plus the Finals Revision Course. Students number 200 each year, achieving 600 in the final year and the Office covers new intake registration plus Oxbridge students.

Main responsibilities

Margaret Garden is responsible for:

- The three employees in her office
- Enrolment documentation
- Timetables for students at each site – colour coding is used for identification
- Student problems. If not doing well they can see their files and pick up report grades – filed alphabetically
- Accommodation difficulties dealt with – some residency given but there can be grant problems
- Elective Period – students offered two months abroad, eg America, and the Medical Office retains contact

General duties

- Filing: Sejal Patel
- Reprography: Sejal Patel
- Stationery: Sue and Diana
- Telephone: all the secretaries
- Travel arrangements – passes and students on Elective Period trips
- Security – records – personal files
- White coats are provided on the purchase of a disc and are returned for cleaning – this involves handling petty cash

Special duties

- Prize-giving and Guest Lecturers – aspects of the work usually carried out by the Dean's Secretary

Facilities

- Electronic typewriters
- Word Processors
- Copiers
- Cabinets – filing alphabetical/numerical for student record cards and reports, accommodation, Elective Periods abroad, etc

Medical secretariat

To provide a service for the consultants there is a secretariat and hospital staff can call on the medical secretaries to carry out work dealing with correspondence, etc, and many use mini audio equipment for their notes and records updating.

Problem areas

The merging of the medical schools has brought about difficulties as there are differing methods of organising work. Other effects have been on promotion and provision of training on the secretarial side, and also limiting staff appraisal and incremental grades.

UNIVERSITY COLLEGE AND MIDDLESEX SCHOOL OF MEDICINE

Photo

Name	No.

Permanent address	Term address

Tel. No.	Tel. No.
Next of kin:	Nationality:	Date of birth:

PREVIOUS EDUCATION
School/Colleges

A LEVELS/PREVIOUS QUALIFICATIONS

Date	Subject	Grade/Class

Local Education Authority:	Fees paid by:

DATE OF ENTRY Preclinical:

Clinical:

TUTOR Preclinical:

Clinical:

EXAMINATION RESULTS

Preclinical examinations	Passed	Failed
Part I Sections A,B,C,		
Part II Sections D,E,F,		
Part III Pharmacology		

Intercalated	B.Sc. degree
Date	Class
Subject	

Final examination	Passed	Failed
Part IV Pathology		
Part V Medicine		
PartVI Clin. Pharmacology		
Part VII Surgery		
Part VIII O & G		

**FINAL QUALIFICATION/
HIGHER DEGREES & DIPLOMAS**   Date

INTERNAL ASSESSMENTS

Date	Subject	Class

STUDENT ASSISTANTSHIPS

Date	Subject	HP/HS	Grade

PRE-REGISTRATION HOUSE APPOINTMENTS

FULL REGISTRATION

CLINICAL APPOINTMENTS

Date From	Date to	Subject	Consultant/Hospital	*Classification

* Key   Grade A - outstanding 5%   Grade C - satisfactory 70%
           Grade B - very good 20%   Grade D - unsatisfactory 5%

PRIZES AND SCHOLARSHIPS

COURSE NOTES

University College & Middlesex School of Medicine

Administration

Vice-Provost (Medical)
Dean
Vice-Dean (Medical)
Sub-Dean & Tutor
Sub-Dean (Curriculum)
Sub-Dean (Postgraduate)
Secretary

The School Office, in liaison with other members of the Administration, is responsible to the Secretary for all matters that concern the clinical medical students as follows:

Liaison with	*School Office*	*Liaison with*
Sub-Dean & Tutor, ie Pastoral care References	Assistant Administrative Secretary: Margaret Garden	Fees Grants
	Student registration and records	
	Courses and timetables	
	Annual reports and general correspondence with Local Education Authorities	
	Lockers and white coats	
	Elective period attachments Elective period grants	
Student Health Care Service	Scholarship awards	Examinations Prizes
	Lecture theatre/tutorial room bookings	
	Residency rooms	
	Student Assistantships	
	General dissemination of information to students	
House Officer Appointments	General Medical Council registration on qualification	Students who are Postgraduate or from Overseas

HOW WOULD YOU DEAL WITH THESE ISSUES?

SECRETARIAL PROCEDURES

12.1 Margaret has the responsibility of organising the distribution of information to each new intake of students who will be going to the Middlesex Hospital, The University Hospital or The Whittington Hospital. She has asked you to think of a clear way of distinguishing students and documents for each Hospital so that the work can be dealt with quickly.

12.2 The secretarial staff are called upon to report to the consultants for dictation. Each consultant has a different method of working and style. Bearing in mind that part of their time is spent in the Medical Office, how would you advise the secretaries to work out their daily schedule of duties?

12.3 There are many documents that have to be completed (eg, Assessment Form pp 100–1). What other methods of collating and storing information could be used in circumstances such as these?

12.4 The Hospital keeps all documentation and stores it in Archives. Bearing in mind that space is expensive in London and that papers can deteriorate, Margaret has been asked to explore and suggest a more durable and suitable method of retaining records and saving space. Prepare a brief report setting out your recommendation and the work that will have to be carried out to put it into effect.

STRUCTURE OF BUSINESS

12.5 The National Health Service and the Private Health Service are run alongside each other in the UK. How are both systems financed and to whom are the administrative managers accountable?

12.6 Why is it necessary for companies to take out insurance and what cover should be made?

12.7 Prepare a draft article on the role of a public relations officer so that information is available in the Medical School Office.

12.8 Efficiency aids the hospitals, administration staff and patients. It is planned to use a consultancy firm to look at the organisation and methods. Margaret requires you to prepare a memorandum to send to the staff, reassuring them and outlining the reasons for this proposal and the type of work that will be carried out. Draft this memorandum.

SECRETARIAL ADMINISTRATION

12.9 Margaret has advised you that there are problems arising from different methods of organising work, eg filing and staff rotas and collection and distribution of mail. Set out your proposed method under each heading and your reasons for the changes you are putting forward.

12.10 Sejal Patel has been promoted from a junior shorthand-typist to secretary to two consultants and her place has to be filled. Draw up a draft advertisement, together with a Job Description, to be passed to the Appointments Section of the Personnel Office.

12.11 Margaret has to consider different ways in which to present statistical data to be used by the hospital staff in articles and reports. On her behalf describe **three** ways in which such data can be presented in an attractive way.

12.12 It is planned to introduce more technology into the Medical School Office. For work to be carried out efficiently in an electronic office, ergonomic features and work flow aspects are important. Under the headings of furniture, equipment, environment and job satisfaction, outline the points you would include in support of the planned changes.

MANAGEMENT APPRECIATION

12.13 In order to successfully control the student intake and the organisation of the course work, Margaret has to devise a student handbook to cover all areas where the students need to be informed and aware. List the points you feel should be included in such a handbook.

12.14 There is a need to advise the medical students about various management aspects of their future employment and you have been asked by Margaret to prepare an information sheet on terms such as job evaluation, merit grading, staff appraisal, organisation charts, functional responsibility, etc. Group these terms appropriately and add any other terms you feel should be included in such an information sheet.

12.15 Staffing is very important in hospitals and every effort is made to obtain staff of the highest calibre in all areas of hospital work.

How can the hospital administration ensure that these high standards are maintained, bearing in mind that as well as permanent staff, a number fall within the category of casual labour?

12.16 The medical secretaries have complained to Margaret that they feel demotivated as they consider their secretarial training is being under-utilised by doctors and consultants. A number of management theorists have written about motivation. Discuss the motivating theories and suggest a possible approach that Margaret might take on behalf of the secretarial staff.

ADDITIONAL STUDENT LEARNING ACTIVITIES

FIND OUT

What changes have taken place in the administration of hospitals?

ROLE PLAY

In pairs act out roles of confidentiality – patients seeking personal information.

Southampton University Faculty of Arts, Department of French

HISTORICAL BACKGROUND

The University owes its origin to the Hartley Institute which was established following a bequest by Henry Robinson Hartley, the son of a Southampton wine merchant, who died in 1850. The Institution, opened in 1862, was intended by Southampton Corporation to be a cultural centre for the townspeople, with a library, museum and lecture halls, but soon began to develop into a teaching college specialising in science and engineering. Towards the end of the century the Hartley College, as it had been renamed, also developed on the Arts side and in 1902 was incorporated under a scheme of the Board of Education as a University College. From this beginning, until the establishment of the University, students read for external degrees of the University of London. The College was accommodated in premises in Southampton High Street, built for the Institution, and remained there until 1919 when it moved to a 54 acre site two miles from the centre of the town. In 1952 the College was constituted by Royal Charter to become the University of Southampton.

There has been an expansion of the University and the late 1950s and 1960s saw a substantial development of the site as departments increased in size and new departments were created. An additional site was purchased to accommodate the new medical school which admitted its first undergraduate students in 1971. In 1986–87 the number of academic and academically-related staff was approximately 1425 and the number of other staff about 1680. There were 6444 full-time and 549 part-time registered students in the eight Faculties: Arts, Science, Engineering and Applied Science, Social Sciences, Educational Studies, Law, Medicine and Mathematical Studies. In addition 1298 students were registered for degrees or other awards regulated through the Board for Collegiate Studies.

The University Charter states that there shall be a Chancellor, up to three Pro-Chancellors and a Vice-Chancellor, plus Deans of Faculties and a Supreme Governing Body of a Court and a Council and Committees. These will consist of members appointed by the public authorities, churches and ex officio members from West Sussex, Wiltshire, Dorset, the Isle of Wight, etc. The Council has the power to manage and regulate the finances of the University and invest any monies belonging to the University.

CASE STUDY ORGANISATION

This case study is concerned with one area of the University, namely the Faculty of Arts, Department of French, where the 320 undergraduates undertake a Four Year Degree Course, one year being spent in France. The Department Head is Professor Michael Kelly and there are 11 Lecturers and 2 Lecteurs from France. The administrative staff consists of Mrs Alison Hamlin with the support of a part-timer.

Professor Kelly, in addition to his Head of Department duties, is also Chairman of the Computing Services Committee and the Network Planning Group for the University.

Communications

Within the University there are numerous means of communication for both the staff and students, the staff receiving a Staff Club Newsletter offering social activities, a New Reporter (see page 109) and Viewpoint publication providing information, plus a comment publication for staff views. These publications are produced within the University by the Public Relations Department and an Editorial Board respectively. The administrative staff also maintain notice-boards for personal messages for students and sections are allocated for specific student groups at various locations. Students can freely seek advice and information from the departmental secretarial staff who offer an 'open door' to their offices.

PERSONNEL ADMINISTRATION

Alison Hamlin is the Departmental Secretary and as such provides secretarial services for Professor Kelly and the other lecturers within the Department. Her role is particularly that of a link between academic staff and students and her time is spent in dealing with administrative/secretarial work for Professor Kelly and handling student queries and any other student matters.

Alison's responsibilities

For Professor Kelly

- dealing with the mail
- correspondence in both French and English
- carrying out work for the other 11 lecturers
- organising meetings
- staff timetable queries
- student records – including essay dates
- telephone calls on 3-person telephone system
- filing
- visitors

- control of stationery and consumables budget
- reprographics (mainly lecture materials)
- travel arrangements

For undergraduate students

- dealing with queries on accommodation
- essay timetables and receiving work for lecturers
- assisting with general information needed
- assisting with requests for changes in the 'hand-in' dates for work (completion of permission forms)

Special duties

- for students studying in France: work schedules – correspondence – messages and solving any problems. Contact being maintained through the Departmental Secretary

- Finalists' Party. An informal graduation party provided by the staff – co-ordinate refreshments and other needs in booked room. Also other occasions, graduation parties, sherry receptions, etc

- Arrangements for visiting lecturers to Department and external examiners – accommodation and any other needs

- Petty cash and consumables budget

- Agree working programme with the part-time member of staff who deals with the UCCA forms (applications for a university place) and assist with photocopying and other work as needed, such as keeping student records up to date

Specific role of departmental secretary

Alison has, as outlined, a secretarial role of dealing with the post and handling correspondence in English and French. She is called upon to answer numerous telephone calls and usually expects a call every 5 minutes. The main concern is that this demand on her time fragments her day and does not allow her to complete a task without interruption, either from the telephone or from visiting students to her office. As Alison's office is opposite the lift, any visitors are also dealt with by her or her colleague. A lot of work is 'on demand' as lecture materials are needed or contact has to be made with staff or students.

Busier times of the year cover registration, the timetable for dissertations, and the updating of record cards where all details are kept of grades, addresses and general comment, as well as the work involved on statistics analysis, study abroad and the requirements of the petty cash, for purchasing equipment and consumables. All financial aspects are on a strictly coded basis and accountable, such as sums of money required from students for photocopying facilities.

Facilities

To assist with the work of the Department there is a dedicated word processor, as well as an electronic typewriter with French language daisy-wheel and code key for accents. In addition the usual photocopying facilities and a 3-person switchboard. Recently introduced is the Minitel providing a continental telephone link with screen for direct messages. This plugs into a telephone socket and will enable lecturers to access facilities on the continent, with messages being displayed on the screen – rather like a Prestel link.

Security is a major concern because personal details of students are not divulged. There are additional security needs in view of the large number of people on the campus requiring care of personal belongings and equipment.

Meetings

The Department holds meetings fortnightly, where the staff discuss administrative matters, course work, forthcoming events and matters concerning the students.

Also there is a Departmental Board Meeting, held termly, attended by all staff and 6 student representatives, where the views of students are sought or student comment needed.

THE BIG LINK-UP TAKES SHAPE

APPROVAL has now been given for the first step towards establishing one of the most modern communications networking systems in any university in the world.

If the five-year plans are approved by Council early next month a university project team will begin working flat out on the proposals at the beginning of August.

Professor Michael Kelly, chairman of the Computing Service Committee and also of the Network Planning Group set up to implement the big link up, says the network will transform the university's teaching and research and will also dramatically increase its administrative efficiency.

Mike told last week's meeting of the Finance and General Purposes Committee, which endorsed his group's proposals, that a fundamental overhaul of the university's communications is not only highly desirable but will in any case soon be inevitable as the existing systems are rapidly becoming overloaded.

"What we are proposing," he told F&GP, "is 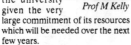 one of the most far-reaching steps the university will take in the next decade. We therefore believe there must be the fullest consideration throughout the university given the very

Prof M Kelly

large commitment of its resources which will be needed over the next few years.

"Despite the cost - which we estimate at £1.7m or more to complete the network - we are convinced that the advantages this technology will give us will keep Southampton in the forefront of university development. We will

by MIKE CHANEY

not only be able to talk to each other more efficiently," he said, "we will be talking to the world."

Mike says he has high hopes that the Computer Board will chip in to help the university establish such a pace-setting system and added that he learned from the UGC team which visited the university earlier this month that the Government has been asked to earmark up to £50m to support the sort of networking proposals Southampton is planning.

Extract from *New Reporter*

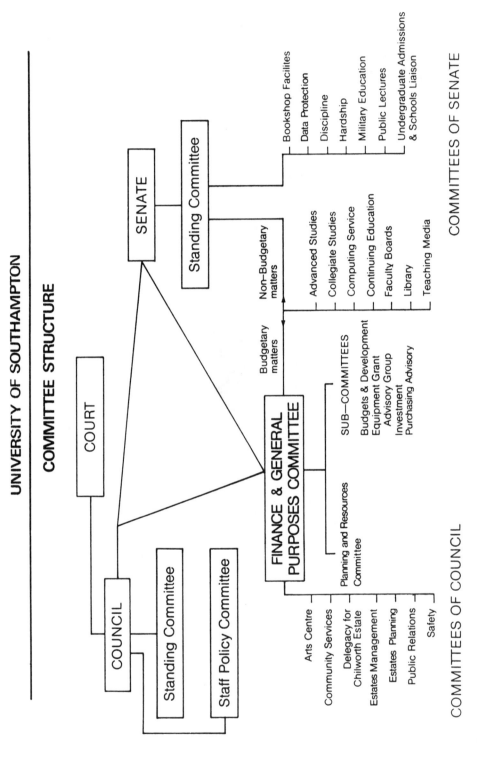

UNIVERSITY OF SOUTHAMPTON

COMMITTEE STRUCTURE

COURT

COUNCIL

SENATE

Standing Committee

Staff Policy Committee

Standing Committee

FINANCE & GENERAL PURPOSES COMMITTEE

Planning and Resources Committee

SUB–COMMITTEES

Budgetary matters

Non-Budgetary matters

Budgets & Development
Equipment Grant
Advisory Group
Investment
Purchasing Advisory

Arts Centre
Community Services
Delegacy for Chilworth Estate
Estates Management
Estates Planning
Public Relations
Safety

Advanced Studies
Collegiate Studies
Computing Service
Continuing Education
Faculty Boards
Library
Teaching Media

Bookshop Facilites
Data Protection
Discipline
Hardship
Military Education
Public Lectures
Undergraduate Admissions & Schools Liaison

COMMITTEES OF COUNCIL

COMMITTEES OF SENATE

WHAT DO YOU KNOW?

SECRETARIAL PROCEDURES

13.1 Alison received a request for the address of an undergraduate in France. How will she tactfully deal with this request and how would you expect her to handle this enquiry?

13.2 Professor Kelly wishes to call a meeting of the Computing Services Committee and has asked Alison to 'organise in the usual way'. What steps will she take to carry out this work?

13.3 Because of pressure of work the stock of Graduate Record Forms has been reduced to a low level. What action can Alison take to control stock levels and ensure this does not happen again?

13.4 As you know, Alison has many interruptions from visitors, undergraduates, telephone calls, etc. Certain qualities will be required to deal with each situation and there are possible ways of organising her time. Suggest how you would deal with such problems.

STRUCTURE OF BUSINESS

13.5 At the end of every course graduates seek employment. If some are initially unsuccessful this indicates an economic problem – why should this be so?

13.6 Which Government Departments are responsible for education and training? Why is there wide representation on the University's Committees?

13.7 In order to prepare a report to justify a requisition for additional equipment and facilities Professor Kelly is considering requests based on one of the following methods:

(*a*) immediate payment
(*b*) hire purchase
(*c*) leasing

and has asked Alison to outline the benefits and drawbacks of each method, explaining which one to recommend. Prepare a draft report for Alison to submit to Professor Kelly.

13.8 The Student Union has decided to debate the question 'What is the present effect of the "cost of living" and "standard of living" on student morale'. What distinguishes these terms and what points do you think will be raised?

SECRETARIAL ADMINISTRATION

13.9 Personal record cards are prepared manually for each graduate giving personal details, grades achieved for course work and any other relevant information. Manually prepared forms are preferred but are time-consuming in updating. What would you list in defence of the retention of this policy and what alternative methods do you consider could be suitable?

13.10 Over the next three months there will be a programme of four visiting French lecturers who will spend 2 days at four different Universities. Prepare a list of possible Universities and a checklist of arrangements to be made. Two lecturers will be accompanied by their wives.

13.11 A member of the University staff is particularly keen on a direct message telephone link with the continent. There are direct message systems, eg through British Telecom. What are the advantages and benefits of such communication links?

13.12 Although budgeting is not a major part of Alison's job as Departmental Secretary, what steps should be taken to control the petty cash and organise the demands on this budget?

MANAGEMENT APPRECIATION

13.13 Bearing in mind the number of Faculties within the University and the size of the staff, communication is a major consideration to ensure a corporate image. Do you think that the publications and noticeboards are sufficient for this purpose and achieve the aim, and what other suggestions can you make?

13.14 Computer Services and Network Planning are areas of work in which Professor Kelly plays a major part. What do you understand by these titles and what benefits do you think will derive from such provisions?

13.15 Any busy office requires a degree of delegation. There are implications involved – how would you define these and ensure successful delegation of work should this office increase its staff?

13.16 Alison has to prepare a statistical analysis of results. Why do organisations require such statistics and surveys carried out and how is this work justified?

ADDITIONAL STUDENT LEARNING ACTIVITIES

FIND OUT

Make enquiries about your local University or Polytechnic and what connections it has with countries in the European Community involving its students, and the subject areas studied. Discuss what benefits you think result from these arrangements.

ROLE PLAY

Assume the role of host/hostess for a visiting businessman and his wife and draw up an itinerary of local places to visit and arrangements to be made, taking account of transport needs and other expenses. In small groups agree an itinerary to include a weekend and one evening for their personal enjoyment and interest, this being their first visit to your area.

Montagu Car Museum

HISTORICAL BACKGROUND

Beaulieu, in Hampshire, has been Lord Montagu's family home since 1538 when, at the Dissolution of the Monasteries by King Henry VIII, Beaulieu Abbey with its 8000 acre estate was purchased from the Crown by his ancestor Thomas Wriothesley, 1st Earl of Southampton. The great Abbey Church and many of the other fine buildings were reduced to ruins, but the Cloisters, Lay Brothers' apartments, Refectory and the two Gatehouses were retained. The Great Gatehouse was turned into a residence and became Palace House, where the family has lived continuously ever since.

In 1951, after Lord Montagu assumed full responsibility for Beaulieu, he decided to open Palace House and its gardens to the public. As a memorial to his father, who was one of the leading pioneers of motoring in Great Britain and the first Parliamentary champion of the motorist's cause, he displayed a handful of early vehicles in the front hall of the house, and it was from this modest beginning that the now world-famous National Motor Museum at Beaulieu grew. Within ten years the collection numbered more than 100 vehicles and by the middle of the 1960s the collection had grown to a point where it was of international significance. The decision to found a charitable trust was taken in 1968 in order to safeguard the museum and the library collections for the long-term benefit of the nation and the trust came into being in 1970.

One of the first tasks of the Trust was to fund and build a new museum and in 1972, under the auspices of the National Motor Museum Trust, the doors of a new 70 000 sq ft museum were opened to the public. The National Motor Museum is a principal feature of the visitor complex at Beaulieu which includes Palace House, Beaulieu Abbey and many special features which follow the motoring theme. Beaulieu is one of Britain's most successful tourist attractions and receives more than 500 000 visitors each year. The National Motor Museum Trust's most recent project was a major new display to mark the Centenary of the Motor Car – 'Wheels, The Legend of the Motor Car' – which was opened by His Royal Highness The Prince of Wales in 1985.

Lord Montagu's current activities

Lord Montagu is Chairman of the Trustees of the National Motor Museum Trust, the Countryside Education Trust, Montagu Ventures Ltd, and Beaulieu Estate and Beaulieu River Management Ltd, all of which are administered at Beaulieu as indicated in the organisation chart on page 118. His other activities include being Chairman of the Historic Buildings and Monuments Commission (English Heritage); a Director of the Mayflower Theatre Trust; Vice President of the Institute of Motor Industry; Chancellor of the Wine Guild of the UK; Fellow of the Royal Society of Arts; President of the Southern Tourist Board; President of the Association of British Transport Museums; President of the English Vineyards Association, and President of the Federation of British Historic Vehicle Clubs.

THE BEAULIEU ORGANISATION

Lord Montagu has defined the overall aim of the activities at Beaulieu and Buckler's Hard as 'to ensure the continued existence and continual enhancement of the Beaulieu Estate as an entity in family ownership, an area of outstanding beauty and an integral part of the New Forest and to make appropriate areas of the Estate accessible for public enjoyment and education'. Some 120 permanent and 180 seasonal staff are employed in the various departments of the Beaulieu organisation with the object of achieving this aim. The Managing Director, Financial Director and the Agent hold senior executive meetings once a week and the Heads of Department with the Managing Director in the chair also meet weekly. These are both informal meetings and no written records are kept.

When staff join the organisation they are issued with a comprehensive staff handbook which contains a history of Beaulieu; the aims and objectives of the organisation; visitor services; rules and conditions of employment; staff services and facilities; departmental organisation; telephone numbers and maps. A weekly bulletin called *Newsline* is distributed to all staff to keep them informed of what is going on and offer relevant information. An annual staff appraisal scheme is operated involving all staff, to review their duties and performance during the preceding year and to discuss and agree changes for the future.

Public relations

The Public Relations Department employs the services of an advertising agency, through whom it handles television and press advertising and the design and production of printed publicity material. Liaison with the travel trade involves attending exhibitions and workshops all over the country to meet tour operators, travel agents, coach companies and Regional and National Tourist Boards to initiate inclusion of Beaulieu and Buckler's Hard in tour programmes, etc. All press matters are handled by the department which is also responsible for the preparation and despatch of press releases for the different events held at Beaulieu. Regular mailings of publicity material are sent to tourist information centres, hotels, camp sites, etc.

LORD MONTAGU'S PRIVATE SECRETARY

Jill Lindemere has been Lord Montagu's Private Secretary for the past sixteen years and she has been actively involved in all of the major developments at Beaulieu since the formation of the National Motor Museum Trust. Lord Montagu spends three days a week in London and, as Chairman of English Heritage, he has a personal assistant and a secretary working for him there. It is, therefore, necessary for the secretaries to liaise on a regular basis to agree dates for appointments, meetings, etc. Jill has an electronic typewriter with full screen facility and access to a copier and fax machine. The fax is particularly useful for transmitting documents to the Personal Assistant in London. Much of Jill's work is done on the telephone, receiving calls for Lord Montagu, making calls for him and arranging meetings, etc. She has two telephone systems: one is a private system with extensions to all members of the family and the other is the system for the whole of the organisation. Jill's other responsibilities include:

- **Personal liaison with Lord Montagu's family**

  Informing members of the family and their secretaries of Lord Montagu's movements and especially his weekend's activities.

- **Meetings**

  Setting up meetings for the Trustees and other bodies by agreeing dates with the participants and arranging the venues.

- **Appointments**

  Arranging appointments and entering them in Lord Montagu's diary and in her own.

- **Invitations**

  Replying to invitations according to the wishes of Lord Montagu and entering the acceptances in the diaries.

- **Filing**

  Filing is arranged alphabetically by subjects within the categories: Beaulieu complex; Museum and Sponsor Companies; Family; Trusts and Associations; Travel; Books and Articles. A rotary-indexing system is used to record names, addresses and telephone numbers in frequent use. Jill finds it useful to have cross-references for individuals and their companies/organisations.

- **Travel arrangements**

  Lord Montagu travels abroad extensively: lecturing in America; participating in veteran and vintage car rallies such as the Australian Bicentennial Rally; holidaying, eg trekking in Nepal. This entails booking air tickets; ordering foreign currency and travellers' cheques; applying for visas; arranging a car to and from the airport and preparing an itinerary (as in the example given on page 119).

- **Typing speeches**

  These are typed with large type on A5 sheets.

- **Arranging business lunches at Palace House**

  After discussion with Lord Montagu Jill is required to telephone the guests' secretaries to agree dates – very often 3–4 months ahead as they are usually important people with full diaries; prepare and send out the invitations with a map of Beaulieu; enter the lunch in the diaries; and notify staff at Beaulieu of the arrangements made.

- **Organising special events**

  Over the years Jill has been responsible for organising various family celebrations and garden parties, eg Lord Montagu's 60th Birthday Party, which nearly 1000 people attended. Her tasks included:

  - compiling and agreeing the guest list with Lord Montagu

  - printing invitation cards, addressing them and sending them out

  - arranging hotel accommodation for the guests

  - liaising with the Catering Manager and other staff at Beaulieu concerning the arrangements to be made. (When arranging special events Jill has to inform the relevant staff at Beaulieu of the day's timetable and the arrangements necessary – an example of a form used for this purpose is given on page 120.)

  - providing Lord Montagu with a final acceptance list, arranged alphabetically

  - after the event, sending out 'thank you' letters for the gifts given to Lord Montagu

  Jill was also given the task of co-ordinating the organisation of an old car rally from London to Brussels to celebrate the UK's entry into the EEC.

- **Arranging social events**

  Lord and Lady Montagu like to visit the theatre and opera and Jill has to obtain the tickets for them and sometimes arrange dinner for the artistes, as on the occasion when members of the Moscow State Ballet visited Beaulieu.

- **Arrangements for the Shooting Season**

  Inviting guests for three separate shoots, arranging for their possible stay in Palace House and consequent dinner parties.

Titles and Forms of Address

During the course of her work Jill has to write to many important and distinguished people and has to be sure that she uses the correct name, title and form of address. To assist her in checking these details she keeps the following books of reference in her office:

Burke's Peerage and Baronetage; Burke's Royal Families of the World; Debrett's Handbook; Debrett's Peerage and Baronetage; Debrett's Correct Form; Directory of Directors; Who's Who; Who's Who in the Motor Industry; Dod's Parliamentary Companion; Spotlight – Actors/Actresses.

Other books which Jill uses in connection with her work include:

Museums Year Book; Directory of Grant Making Trusts; Roget's Thesaurus of English Words and Phrases; Historic Houses Trade Manual; Historic Houses, Castles and Gardens; World Atlas.

Press relations

Although the Public Relations Manager normally deals with press relations, Jill has occasions when she has to deal with telephone calls from the press, radio and television when reporters ask to speak to Lord Montagu. Examples are when he was being questioned about the hippies' presence at Stonehenge (in his capacity as Chairman of English Heritage) and in the controversy over rumours of the European Community banning cars over 20 years old. Jill's advice when dealing with reporters is:

- be approachable, friendly and cooperative
- allow your employer time to prepare his/her response
- if information is freely available, give it without 'hedging'
- guard against divulging any information which is secret or confidential

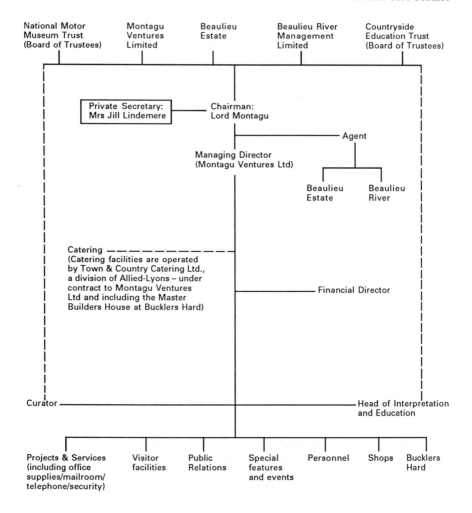

National Motor   Montagu   Beaulieu   Beaulieu River   Countryside
Museum Trust   Ventures   Estate   Management   Education Trust
(Board of Trustees) Limited   Limited   (Board of Trustees)

Private Secretary: Chairman:
Mrs Jill Lindemere   Lord Montagu

                                              Agent

                     Managing Director
                     (Montagu Ventures Ltd)

                                        Beaulieu   Beaulieu
                                        Estate   River

Catering
(Catering facilities are operated
by Town & Country Catering Ltd.,
a division of Allied-Lyons – under
contract to Montagu Ventures   Financial Director
Ltd and including the Master
Builders House at Bucklers Hard)

Curator   Head of Interpretation
                                                   and Education

Projects & Services   Visitor   Public   Special   Personnel   Shops   Bucklers
(including office   facilities   Relations   features   Hard
supplies/mailroom/   and events
telephone/security)

Organisation Chart

Lord Montagu's Itinerary
Australian Bicentennial Rally
20th February – 21st March 1988
(with HRH Prince Michael of Kent)

Monday 22 Feb	c/o Mark Babidge, Bond Corporation, Perth	
	tel 9– 325 4555	
till:		
Sunday 28 Feb	**Rally starts:**	
Sunday 28 Feb	Merredin, W. A.	(Potts Motor Inn)
Monday 29 Feb	Kalgoorlie, W. A.	(Overland Motel)
Tuesday 1 March	Balladonia, W. A.	(Balladonia Hotel)
Wednesday 2 March	Eucla, W. A.	(Amber Motel)
Thursday 3 March	Ceduna, S. A.	(Community Hotel)
Friday 4 March	Ceduna – rest day	(Community Hotel)
Saturday 5 March	Port Augusta, S. A.	(Acacia Ridge Motor Inn)
Sunday 6 March	**Adelaide**	
staying:	Flinders Lodge Motel	
	tel 8– 332 8222	
till:		
Wednesday 9 March	Bordertown, S. A.	(Dukes Motor Inn)
Thursday 10 March	Ballarat, Vic.	(Old Ballarat Village)
Friday 11 March	Ballarat, Vic.	(Old Ballarat Village)
Saturday 12 March	Seymour, Vic.	(Coach & Bushmans Inn)
Sunday 13 March	Beechworth, Vic.	(Armour Motor Inn)
Monday 14 March	Tumut, N. S. W.	(Motel Farrington)
Tuesday 15 March	**Canberra**	
	Staying at Government House	
	Rally remains in Canberra till:	

Sunday 20 March: am   Final Awards – leave for London.

NB: *Telephone code* for Australia is 010 61.
    Perth is 8 hours ahead of GMT, *Adelaide* 10½, *Canberra* 11.

SPECIAL VISIT INFORMATION SHEET

NAME OF ORGANISATION: SOUTHAMPTON CITIZEN OF THE YEAR AWARD

NAME OF CONTACT: MR ALAN COOMBES

DATE OF VISIT: MONDAY 8 AUGUST 19--   **NO IN PARTY:** 2

TIME OF ARRIVAL: 12.00 NOON   **TIME OF DEPARTURE:**

METHOD OF TRANSPORT: OWN   **WHOM TO MEET:**
                                              LESLEY HARNETT OR
METHOD OF PAYMENT: COMPLIMENTARY   DONNA SURPLICE

REASON FOR VISIT: SOUTHAMPTON CITIZEN OF THE YEAR - VIP VISIT
                       TO BEAULIEU

TIMED ITINERARY

12.00 noon   Arrival in the Information Centre.
                Donna or Lesley from PR to greet. (Information
                Hostess to call PR Dept on arrival of guests.)

12.15 pm   Guided tour of the National Motor Museum please
                and ride on 'Wheels'.

1.15 pm   Free time for guests to have lunch in Brabazon.
                (Not complimentary.)

2.00 pm   Free time to look around complex and Abbey, ride
                on Monorail, Miniature Railway World, etc.

3.00 pm   Guided tour of Palace House please.

4.00 pm   Tea with Lord Montagu in private apartments please.

SPECIAL REQUIREMENTS:

QUESTION TIME AT BEAULIEU

SECRETARIAL PROCEDURES

14.1 Select eight of the reference books kept by Jill and explain, with examples, what use they would be to her.

14.2 Outline the topics which the Personnel Department should include in an induction course for new staff. What are the benefits of such a course to (*a*) the employer and (*b*) the employees?

14.3 In what circumstances would each of the following documents be used at Beaulieu:

(*a*) Inventory
(*b*) Delivery note
(*c*) P45
(*d*) Credit note
(*e*) Stock requisition
(*f*) Paying-in slip?

14.4 Suggest in what ways Lord Montagu's Private Secretary might communicate with:

(*a*) A manager whose work takes him to all parts of the visitors' complex;
(*b*) The Personal Assistant in London;
(*c*) All secretaries engaged at Beaulieu;
(*d*) Lord Montagu travelling by car in the South of France?

STRUCTURE OF BUSINESS

14.5 Why is the tourist industry important for a country's prosperity? What factors are likely to deter tourists from visiting Britain and how can they be remedied?

14.6 Discuss the role and importance of the Public Relations Department at Beaulieu. What are the advantages of using an advertising agency?

14.7 Improvements in efficiency may be gained through the use of:

(*a*) new technology
(*b*) organisation and methods survey
(*c*) periodic staff training

What do you understand by each of these terms and how could they improve efficiency at Beaulieu?

14.8 In what ways do local and central government influence the administration of the Beaulieu organisation?

SECRETARIAL ADMINISTRATION

14.9 Assume that you are working as Lord Montagu's Personal Assistant in London. What arrangements would you make to liaise with Jill at Beaulieu and what matters would you need to discuss with her?

14.10 Prepare a draft press release for the Public Relations Department on the visit of the Moscow State Ballet to Beaulieu.

14.11 Draw up a checklist of the arrangements you would make to co-ordinate the organisation of the Old Car Rally from London to Brussels.

14.12 Provide a detailed list of the contents for the staff handbook and explain how the employees and employer benefit from its use.

MANAGEMENT APPRECIATION

14.13 (*a*) Compare Lord Montagu's aims for the Beaulieu organisation with those of an industrial organisation.
(*b*) Suggest what objectives should be set for the Financial Director in order to meet these aims.

14.14 Discuss the manner in which the Managing Director communicates with senior executives and heads of department. Are there any advantages in keeping written records of his meetings?

14.15 If the Beaulieu organisation decided to invest in a major programme of computerisation, what advantages would be gained and what possible effects would it have on employees?

14.16 Explain briefly what you understand by the following management functions and relate them to the Managing Director's role at Beaulieu:

(*a*) organisation
(*b*) direction
(*c*) control
(*d*) delegation.

ADDITIONAL STUDENT LEARNING ACTIVITIES

FIND OUT

How would you address letters to Lord Montagu and Prince Michael of Kent, who are Trustees of the National Motor Museum?

ROLE PLAY

Jill's telephone conversation with a reporter concerning Lord Montagu's reactions to the hippies' presence at Stonehenge. Lord Montagu is away at the time.

Tate & Lyle PLC

HISTORICAL BACKGROUND

The Tate & Lyle family of companies originated from the amalgamation in 1921 of the long-established sugar and syrup refining businesses of Henry Tate and Abram Lyle. These had begun when, in 1865, Abram Lyle built a refinery at Greenock and in 1873 Henry Tate built his first sugar refinery at Liverpool. From these roots it has grown and diversified to become an international Group operating in over 40 countries around the world. The success story of this company has been evolutionary, with its entry into cane sugar production in Jamaica and Trinidad and the successful campaign of 'Mr Cube' created to combat nationalisation threats in the UK in 1949. Sugar Line was formed as a joint venture shipping company with the United Molasses Company in 1951, and in 1959 the controlling interest in the Canada and Dominion Sugar Company (now Redpath Industries Ltd) was obtained. In the 1960s Sugar Line became a wholly-owned subsidiary of Tate & Lyle and in 1963 further expansion saw the company move into the Belize Sugar Industries. In 1966 United Molasses joined the Group, and the shipping company Athel Line was then acquired. The 1970s brought expansion into the starch and chemical industries and into the European Economic Community.

Rationalisation of UK sugar refining operations took place in 1979–83, with a disposal programme of certain Group assets. In 1981 the Company introduced an employee share option scheme.

Acquisitions followed in 1983–1988, with control of the Portuguese Sugar Refining Company, which involved raising £41m through a rights issue, and the purchase of six beet sugar factories in mid-west USA in 1985 (since added to). Another Portuguese refinery was acquired, plus diversifying in Canada and the USA into Texas Plastic Industries and Arbor Plastic Products Inc.

Over the next few years the Group plans to develop further its worldwide businesses in traditional sweeteners and new calorie-free sweeteners; in molasses and speciality animal feeds and, in Northern America, in the supply of plastic products to the automotive and construction industries. The Group plans to seek new areas for the logical extension of its business activities and to achieve steady growth in the global market. Today the Tate & Lyle Group provides a livelihood for many thousands of people around the world and produces a turnover in excess of one and a half billion pounds.

Organisation

The Board of Directors reflects the growth and history of the company, with the Chairman and Chief Executive, Mr Neil Shaw, originally joining Canada and Dominion Sugar Company and holding a variety of management positions with the Group before succeeding Sir Robert Haslam in 1986. Other directors have worked in Canada and the USA, and the non-executive directors have experience in fields such as Allied-Lyons Plc, the TSB and Reed International. It is interesting to record that the founding families are currently represented by Saxon Tate and that in 1978 John Lyle held the Chairmanship.

The Board has six non-executive directors who provide knowledge, objectivity and balance to an extent which might not be available if the Board consisted only of full-time executives. These non-executive directors, through membership of the Audit Committee, monitor the Company's internal control procedures and, through membership of the Remuneration Committee, approve the salaries and conditions of employment of the executive directors and also advise the Chairman and top management on management structure and succession planning.

CASE STUDY

The member of staff chosen for this case study is Miss Sylvia Hennen, who holds the position of Secretary and Personnel Officer and works for the Administration and Personnel Manager. She is responsible for the office juniors, and also for the directors' secretaries.

Sylvia Hennen can call on a great deal of experience having worked at secretarial level for Chairmen and Managing Directors of nationally recognised companies such as Seagrams, Bovril and Bambergers. She has also experienced redundancy and changes in her employment and has moved from a purely secretarial job to be Secretary and Personnel Officer at Tate & Lyle PLC.

Her main duties

- The recruitment of all secretaries and staff up to junior management level
- Responsibility for the administration of the company's private health scheme
- Supervision of staff for whom she is responsible
- Dealing with personnel problems of all staff up to junior management level

General duties

- All secretaries undertake their own filing; reprography; telephoning; organising travel arrangements; and correspondence/mail

Special duties

- Organising evening parties for staff on the Company's sixteenth-century barge on the Thames on behalf of the Chairman

Facilities

- All secretaries use word processors; photocopiers; electronic typewriters; and microfiche readers and printers

Training

- As Sylvia Hennen's work combines secretarial with personnel work she is involved in interviewing, meetings and management training courses. These courses are held in country hotels, and candidates are selected by the Group Personnel Development Manager as having future promotion potential

- Other courses cover Report Writing, Negotiating Skills, Presentation Skills, etc and these are arranged at the company's premises in Cadogan Square

Personnel organisation

The size of Tate & Lyle dictates the need for a detailed organisation chart (*see* page 126) and specific responsibilities are held by members of staff, such as:

- Control of stationery: Purchasing Officer

- Telecommunications: Group Management Services Department

- Mail: Services Supervisor

- Training: Group Personnel Department

- Security/Safety, etc: Administration Manager

- Job evaluation: Administration Manager

- Management training: Group Personnel Department

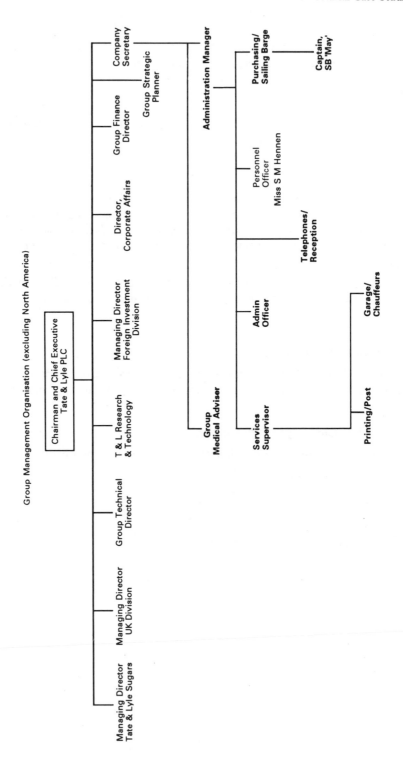

Group Management Organisation (excluding North America)

WHAT IS YOUR OPINION?

SECRETARIAL PROCEDURES

15.1 Sylvia Hennen is arranging an Induction Programme for recently appointed junior staff and has asked you to draft a One-Day Programme to include all relevant areas that need to be covered for the new employee.

15.2 In your work you sometimes deal with confidential matters. How will Sylvia advise you to

(*a*) ensure that filed copies remain inaccessible to unauthorised persons

(*b*) deal with colleagues who ask direct questions about such confidential matters

(*c*) ensure that visitors to your office do not see this work?

15.3 Tate & Lyle PLC use microfiche readers and printers. Why and for what purposes do you think such equipment is used?

15.4 As Tate & Lyle PLC has diversified into a number of different business areas, eg sweeteners, plastics, ships, etc, how would you organise the filing system and classify correspondence?

STRUCTURE OF BUSINESS

15.5 The financial state of affairs of the company is given in the balance sheet which contains reference to fixed assets, current assets, current liabilities and capital employed. A new employee has asked you to explain these terms to her.

15.6 The Tate & Lyle PLC company has a wide interest in a range of products and markets. Reference is often made to 'the marketing mix'. What do you understand by this term?

15.7 In preparation for a Training Programme for new staff you have been asked to draft course notes to explain 'The functioning of the Public Limited Company'. What part is played by shareholders, directors, debenture holders and management?

15.8 In 1949 there were proposals to nationalise Tate & Lyle. Why do you think the Government of the day proposed this action and why did the Company organise a campaign against it and introduce 'Mr Cube'?

SECRETARIAL ADMINISTRATION

15.9 A number of management training courses are run by the company and some assessment is required of the lecturers' performance and of the accommodation provided. Devise a suitable questionnaire and state the basic principles of form design.

15.10 Sylvia has the responsibility of organising an evening party on the Company's barge on the Thames. As she will be away for a short time on business she has asked you to undertake the provisional arrangements.
Prepare a checklist for yourself on the action you will take on her behalf and the order in which the arrangements should be made.

15.11 Senior secretaries face problems of 'prioritising' their work and dealing with the pressures and demands on their time. Can Time Management help and what other assistance can be given?

15.12 Word processing plays a major role in the modern office. What facilities are now available and how has this technology helped the Tate & Lyle administrative staff?

MANAGEMENT APPRECIATION

15.13 Tate & Lyle PLC offer a number of courses for management staff. Why do you think emphasis is placed on Report Writing, Negotiating Skills, Presentation Skills, etc? What other aspects of management training do you think would be included?

15.14 The company has diversified into many product areas. State your understanding of the reasons for this action and its effect on the staff and the company as a whole.

15.15 The Board of Directors consists of Executive and Non-Executive Directors. Describe the functions of the Directors and elaborate on the Tate & Lyle view that non-executive directors provide 'knowledge, objectivity and balance'.

15.16 To motivate staff, companies provide rewards, facilities, communication channels, etc. Why is it necessary for management to devote time and money to this?

ADDITIONAL STUDENT LEARNING ACTIVITIES

FIND OUT

Take another well-known company and try to establish, through reference sources, product areas in which your chosen company is involved.

ROLE PLAY

In small groups of two or three, create an interviewing panel and candidate for junior and senior clerical-secretarial posts.

Draper Tools Limited

The role and responsibilities of Joan Cuthbert as a Senior Secretary at Draper Tools Ltd is the focal point of this case study set against the background of a very successful private business, marketing hand, power and precision tools throughout the United Kingdom and Eire.

COMPANY BACKGROUND

Mr Bert Draper formed the company in 1919 and within a year he had established himself at Kingston-on-Thames in a tool business which was to become one of the most successful in its field. In 1936 Bert's son Norman, then fifteen years old, joined the firm as a van boy and at the end of his first week at work was selling tools from a second-hand van. Now he is Chairman of the company and, with his son John (who joined the firm in 1970), Joint Managing Director of what has become a multi-million pound company. The company eventually outgrew its Kingston premises and a lack of suitable sites forced the company to look further afield and in 1962 it took over the site of a former Royal Navy Victualling Depot in Hampshire. It has remained a private family business for three generations. Today Mr Norman Draper and his son John retain their belief in what they describe as old fashioned virtues of good service and quality products at affordable prices, but also recognise the need to move with new technology and a changing market.

COMPANY ORGANISATION

Drapers does not manufacture tools but orders them in bulk from factories in this country and throughout the world, particularly West Germany and Japan. Some products are marketed under the maker's own name but many are packaged and sold under the Draper banner. Ninety-nine per cent of Draper's sales outlets are through the retail trade, ranging from the small corner shop to the large multiples such as Woolworths. They do very little direct selling to consumers, apart from very large companies such as British Leyland, Ford and General Motors who only consider buying in bulk.

At the Head Office, where 220 staff are employed (including 85 administrative and sales personnel), order processing, despatch and stocktaking have been improved with the introduction of computer-aided design and an expanded mainframe computer system, which speeds accounting, stock movement and sales analysis. The modern 2250 square metre open plan general office houses the latest developments in computer communications, with sales personnel having direct access to all relevant information. Although individual very well appointed offices have been provided for the joint managing directors they prefer to work in the open plan office to be more accessible and in close touch with all staff.

An enlarged warehousing complex of over 17 500 square metres enables the company to purchase and store larger and more varied stocks of tools. Ninety-seven per cent of the range is available ex-stock. New tools are continually being added to the already vast product range of over 14 500 items. These include power tools, gardening tools, hand tools and specialist products such as the Draper Expert range which is tailored for the professional market. Draper Tools is also the sole concessionaire in the United Kingdom and Eire for the West German manufacturers of 'Metabo' power tools, 'Elora' spanners and wrenches and 'Knipex' pliers and cutters.

The marketing centre at Head Office incorporates demonstration and training areas. Courses for customers' shop staff are held regularly with Draper's experts giving guidance on merchandising and stock display. The company employs a team of 60 representatives and merchandising staff throughout the country. The company has stands at most major exhibitions to promote its products to both trade customers and consumers. The in-house printing section is part of an extensive publicity department with its own designers, artists, photographer and typesetting personnel who are responsible for producing company sales literature, packaging and advertising. Sports sponsorship forms an integral part of the company's publicity campaign to promote the company's name and products. The Draper name is associated with most of the large audience sports in the UK and Ireland, ensuring strong brand recognition for their products. Sponsorships include First Division Southampton Football Club, Motor Racing and the Draper Solent Stars Basketball Team.

The company uses a variety of delivery methods to ensure that orders arrive on time. These include an efficient nationwide delivery service, Royal Mail and the company's own delivery vehicles.

THE SECRETARY'S ROLE AND RESPONSIBILITIES

Joan Cuthbert is Secretary to Mr John Draper, Joint Managing Director, and Mr Terry Cornwall, Sales Director, and has responsibility for a junior secretary who assists her. The organisation chart on page 132 shows her position in the company and the departmental structure.

Joan is responsible for:

- **Secretarial duties for her directors**. These include shorthand and audio typing, telephone communications and receiving visitors

- **The office diary and making appointments**. The directors keep their own diaries but Joan tries to monitor their activities in an office diary. When making appointments it is normally necessary for her to make a provisional booking and confirm it in writing later when the director has been consulted

- **Open and distribute the incoming mail**

- **Travel arrangements**. This entails booking flights through a local travel agency and typing itineraries

- **Correspondence received from outside sales staff**. These staff do not have secretarial facilities on the spot and use Head Office for any typing tasks

- **Customer queries and preparation and distribution of sales letters**. See specimen letter on page 133. Top copies with personalised details are always sent to potential customers

- **Exhibition arrangements**. These include booking hotels and providing a telephone link with staff on the stand. Joan is presently considering using the fax service for these communications

- **Recruitment, selection and employment of office staff**. This involves drafting and inserting advertisements in local newspapers, collating replies for consideration by managers, inviting applicants for interview and arranging the interviews, interviewing applicants and preparing contracts of employment. Rates of pay are determined by the directors

Joan's assistant deals with the filing, telephoning, copying and the more routine typing and clerical duties.

Office services

The firm's incoming and outgoing mail is handled by clerical staff who take turns in working in the postroom and a manager sorts the post for distribution to departments. The Buying Department deals with the purchasing and control of office stationery supplies. A tannoy system is operated from the reception office to make contact with personnel throughout the office and warehouse buildings. Management communicate information to staff by means of a twice weekly staff memo. Very few meetings take place and those that are held are usually of an impromptu nature to co-ordinate the views of a group of people.

Plans for the future

The company's plans for the future involve an expansion of its head office complex so that it can store and supply an even greater product range and further increase customer services to meet the challenge of the 1990s.

Draper Tools Limited

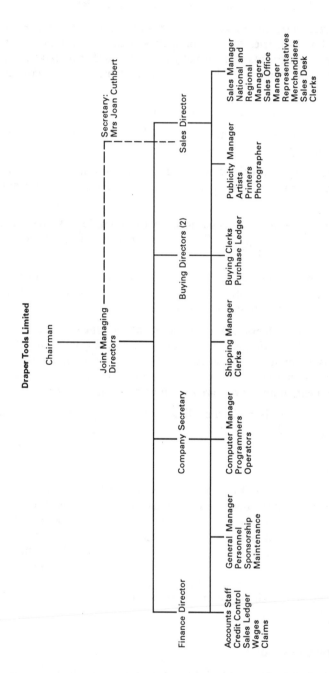

Chairman

Joint Managing Directors — — — — — — — Secretary: Mrs Joan Cuthbert

Finance Director | Company Secretary | Buying Directors (2) | Sales Director

Accounts Staff
Credit Control
Sales Ledger
Wages
Claims

General Manager
Personnel
Sponsorship
Maintenance

Computer Manager
Programmers
Operators

Shipping Manager
Clerks

Buying Clerks
Purchase Ledger

Publicity Manager
Artists
Printers
Photographer

Sales Manager
National and
Regional
Managers
Sales Office
Manager
Representatives
Merchandisers
Sales Desk
Clerks

Draper Tools Ltd Hursley Road Chandlers Ford Hampshire SO5 5YF
Tel.(0703) 266355 International Tel.+44 703 266355
Telex 47686 Fax (0703) 260784

REF: D23
Date

Name and Address

Dear Sirs,

Account No. A12345

Following the recent visit of our Area Sales Representative, we would like
to confirm that we have now opened an account for you and we set out below
the terms which are applicable to your company.   As we are offering you
our best retail terms available, these terms are subject to a six months
trial period, after which time we will review the situation:

DRAPER Products   - X%

METABO Products   - Y%

Nett monthly account.
Payment by the 20th of the month following date of invoice.

We are pleased to confirm the above terms to the following conditions:

1)   We expect a minimum average turnover of £0000.00 per month nett.

2)   Your account must be maintained within our terms of business as laid
      down in the current price list.

3)   These terms would be subject to an annual review.

4)   Should you fail to achieve your target, we will give you three months
      notice before implementing your new terms.

Should you have any queries regarding the above, then please do not
hesitate to contact the undersigned.

Assuring you of our best attention at all times, we remain,

Yours faithfully,
DRAPER TOOLS LIMITED

Sales Manager

Registered Office: Hursley Road Chandlers Ford Hampshire SO5 5YF   Registered in England No.570630

DECISION TIME

SECRETARIAL PROCEDURES

16.1 How would you suggest that Joan should monitor her directors' activities more closely to avoid having to make provisional appointments. She would like to keep an accurate and full record in the office diary of the movements of all directors. What could she do to facilitate this?

16.2 Mr John Draper has to visit a company in Japan. Describe four important formalities (apart from the mode of travel itself) that his secretary must ensure are completed before departure.

16.3 The sales representatives post hand-written documents to Head Office for typing and it is slow and unreliable. In a memo to Mr T Cornwall put forward two alternative methods for improving the speed and efficiency of the typing service for sales representatives.

16.4 (a) Explain the steps you would take to prepare the sales letters which are 'top copies and personalised'.
(b) What sources of reference would you use to find the names and addresses of hardware merchants and DIY stores?
(c) How would you record the results of these letters?

STRUCTURE OF BUSINESS

16.5 How does a private limited company, such as Draper Tools, differ from a public limited company?

16.6 Most of Draper's sales outlets are through the retail trade, from the small corner shop to the large multiples and everything in between. What is 'in between'? How have retailing methods changed in recent years?

16.7 Draper is the 'middleman' or wholesaler operating between manufacturers and retailers. In what ways do the manufacturers and retailers benefit from the existence of wholesalers?

16.8 Draper attaches a great deal of importance to advertising and sales promotion and devote considerable financial resources to them. What do you think it expects from this large expenditure and how can it be justified?

SECRETARIAL ADMINISTRATION

16.9 Draper's open plan office houses the latest developments in computer communications with sales personnel having direct access to all relevant information. Describe these developments and say what type of information sales personnel would require.

16.10 The Training Manager of a large chain of shops has asked Drapers to provide a one-day merchandising training course for their sales assistants.

(a) Draw up a checklist of the arrangements which Joan would need to make for this course, indicating when action would be initiated;
(b) Write a letter to the Training Manager confirming the arrangements made.

16.11 Would you advise Joan to use the fax service for a communication link with staff on exhibition stands? Suggest how the fax service could be used in other ways at Draper's Head Office.

16.12 Joan is required to draw up a briefing sheet for staff involved in the recruitment and employment of staff. Suggest what information she should give under the following headings:

(a) drafting advertisements
(b) shortlisting
(c) interviewing

MANAGEMENT APPRECIATION

16.13 Discuss the Draper philosophy of providing good service and quality products at affordable prices but recognising the need to move with new technology and a changing market. Is there any conflict here with the motive of running a business to make a profit?

16.14 Comment on the Joint Managing Directors' style of management in which they work in the open plan office to be more accessible and in close touch with all staff.

16.15 What advice would you give to Joan with regard to the legal requirements in the drafting of advertisements?

16.16 Discuss the importance of meetings as a means of communication, control and innovation in business. What are the advantages and disadvantages of formal meetings as compared with the informal 'impromptu' meetings, such as those held at Draper?

ADDITIONAL STUDENT LEARNING ACTIVITIES

FIND OUT

the names of six other firms which sponsor large audience sports and for each state:

(a) the type of business unit
(b) the products sold
(c) the sport sponsored.

ROLE PLAY

a presentation to a local school given by two representatives of Draper Tools to explain what the firm does, how it markets its products and what its plans are for the future.

Prima magazine

Prima is owned by Gruner & Jahr, a German publishing company, and published in the UK by G & J (UK). *Prima* operates from a large office block in Central London along with *Best*, another of the company's magazines.

DEE'S SECRETARIAL CAREER PROGRESSION

Dee Saker began working for *Prima* in February 1986 as Personal Assistant to the Editor, Sue James, when the first edition of the magazine was being put together. Throughout her career Dee had always been interested in fashion and was keen to be associated with it in her work. After attending a fashion merchandising course at the College for the Distributive Trades, she started work as a sales assistant with Country Casuals and was soon promoted to assistant manageress and later manageress of a fashion showroom involving an element of office administration. She realised that she would require more knowledge and skills in administration to make further progress in her career, so she attended a year's TOPS course in typing, audio-typing, word processing, shorthand and secretarial practice. Her first experience of working with a magazine was with Business Press, a section of the IPC Group, as secretary to the Advertisement Manager of *Motor Trader*, a trade paper, and this gave her a 'foot in the door' to return to her interest in fashion. It was not long before she became secretary to the Fashion Editor of *Woman's Own*, which provided ideal experience in preparation for the wider responsibilities of her present job.

PRIMA'S AIMS

Prima aims not only to entertain but to inform and inspire its readers. Its editorial approach is always friendly but not too cosy, authoritative but never condescending.

Prima covers the full range of classic women's interests:

- fashion for all ages and sizes

- homecraft from embroidery to DIY
- knitting – hand, machine and crochet
- cookery – step by step to collectable cookcards
- general features on women's health, children, legal matters, travel, pets and gardening

The magazine is informative and entertaining with plenty of practical tips. In addition, there is the unique Prima Pattern – a pull-out sewing pattern sheet that is easy and simple to follow. Each month there is a new garment to sew as well as knitting and embroidery charts.

Prima is designed for the woman who:

- is active in her own life and that of her family
- controls the household budget
- manages the family's life
- needs products which give satisfaction and save time
- welcomes ideas for things to do, to make and to buy

The following are recent circulation figures of *Prima*, and the corresponding figures of the total women in the UK:

	Prima readers	**All women in UK**
January – June 1987	1 649 000	23 210 000
July – December 1987	1 973 000	23 286 000
January – June 1988	2 139 000	23 379 000

Source: National Readership Survey

Circulation figures of the magazine are monitored closely to identify trends and assess progress. The figures are collected and certified by the Audit Bureau of Circulations (ABC).

PA'S ROLE AND RESPONSIBILITIES

Prima employs 40 people in its London Office. A section of the company's organisation chart is illustrated on page 142. Dee is responsible for the Junior Editorial Assistant, Tara Sloggett, who assists her and works in the same office, which is situated next to the Editor's office. They use electronic typewriters and have access to a copier and fax facilities. Management is looking into the possibility of using desktop publishing. The day begins at 1000 and ends at 1800, although Dee's hours have to be flexible to cater for unexpected exigencies.

Dee's main responsibilities are listed in the job description on page 141. Much of her work is done on the telephone and revolves around the many meetings which are held. Dee is the one person, apart from the Editor, who liaises with staff throughout *all* stages of magazine production. She ensures that copy is passed through the organisation and liaises with managerial PAs in organising production meetings. She is also responsible for organising a

'Think Tank' twice a year for all editorial heads, which is a conference for discussing future ideas and promotions. A wall chart is used to monitor the progress of each monthly edition of the magazine.

It is proposed to introduce a staff appraisal scheme in the near future.

Correspondence

Dee sorts the mail and decides which letters should be seen by the Editor and which she can answer herself on behalf of the Editor (*see* example on page 143) or pass on to others to deal with. As the Editor spends much of her time attending meetings, there is little time for her to deal with correspondence but Dee makes sure that urgent mail reaches her and arranges dictation sessions with her at least once a week for the less urgent matters. It is Dee's responsibility to prompt her about matters requiring attention. The Editor's mailbag might, for example, contain:

- literature relating to new products such as cosmetics, holidays, garden furniture, etc
- invitations to attend the launch of a new book, perfume, etc
- requests from readers for further information about products featured in *Prima*
- offers to write articles for *Prima*
- queries concerning magazine subscription rates

Sue James, Editor of *Prima* (left) talking over a point in the mail with her PA, Dee Saker.

- notices of meetings
- requests for help from readers using patterns
- memos concerning production problems, eg when there is a revised schedule for receipt of material
- notices of film screenings
- a letter from a reader whose photograph of her pet had gone astray in the post
- letters congratulating the Editor on the quality of the magazine

Some time ago the Editor received several letters from readers objecting to cigarette advertising. Some readers said that they contradicted the advice given in the magazine on healthy living and, as a result, the magazine no longer accepts such advertisements.

The PA's daily routine

Although two days are never the same in an editor's office, there are certain tasks which must be done daily, for example:

- Compare the Editor's diary with her own and make any necessary entries
- Read, sort and distribute the post
- Assemble files and papers required for the day and place them in the Editor's 'in-tray'
- Make travel arrangements for the Editor
- Answer the telephone and type dictated correspondence
- Deal with routine letters
- Anticipate the Editor's needs and supply her with any information she needs

Dee keeps two diaries – the Editor's and her own (see specimen pages of Dee's diary below). The Editor takes her diary with her wherever she goes and Dee has to rescue it at frequent intervals to bring it up to date.

DIARY

Monday 1 August 19––

Arrange lunch for Sue, Editorial Director and Deputy Editor

Ring Ian Jackson

Sue: Harbin contract to be signed for special offer

1100   Sue: Meeting with Advertisement Director and Features Editor

1500   Sue: Live interview for Radio Bedford re Jubilee House

1745   Meeting with Sue

Tuesday 2 August 19—

Write to Royal School of Needlework

1000 Correspondence with Sue – NB: Memo required to Features Editor re motoring policy

1100 Sue: Interviews for Deputy Features Editor

1200 Conference with all Editorial Section Heads to discuss future issues – ideas and promotions

1630 Sue: Look at photographs for November edition with Art Director

1800 Sue: Press Reception for launch of new book at Covent Garden

Wednesday 3 August 19—

Arrange discussion for a possible Save the Children *Prima* Christmas Tree Project

Update organisation chart

1030 Sue: Meeting with Patterns Department re December's patterns

1300 Sue: Lunch with Gordon Russell, Director of PR Company (prepare client list)

1600 Sue: Fashion meeting

Following through the editor's initiatives

Dee has to follow through the Editor's initiatives, providing her with the necessary information and arranging meetings with appropriate departmental heads. For example, the Editor might ask her to follow up a project on children's videos which will involve researching videos, contacting the publishers and arranging for the videos to be reviewed.

The Editor might want to see the New York fashion collections, leaving Dee to find out flight times, suitable hotels, where and when the shows are taking place, and the important publishers to meet whilst she is in New York. Dee would liaise with the company's office in New York when making these enquiries, preparing a detailed itinerary for the Editor before she left.

On one occasion Dee had planned a business trip to France for the Editor and had arranged for her to carry out a consumer test on a camera at the same time. The manufacturer had been requested to supply a camera to the office, but failed to deliver it until five minutes after Sue had left. Frantic steps had to be taken to ensure that Sue received the camera before she left the country!

Dee was given the task of organising *Prima*'s First Birthday Party. She was given a budget and left to select a good hotel venue; choose the menu;

design, print and distribute the invitation cards and follow up replies; arrange for speeches and their timing; decide whether to have music and, if so, what music; and arrange the tables, microphone, etc.

The magazine is currently involved in a project to help mentally handicapped teenagers by decorating and furnishing a flat which has been given to Jubilee House, a respite home, by the local council at Welwyn Garden City. The Editor visited the flat and arranged for it to be painted by *Prima* and for various firms, associated with the magazine, to furnish it. An official opening of the flat has been arranged and Dee has been asked to send out invitations to the people who have donated items for it.

Dee organises the travel arrangements for photographic trips and visits to exhibitions in this country and abroad. Recently she arranged for the models, photographers, fashion editors and make-up artist to visit a resort in the Algarve by negotiating a special discount rate in return for a mention on the editorial pages. Dee sometimes attends press receptions on behalf of the Editor and in so doing makes contacts for future magazine projects.

JOB DESCRIPTION

Job Title: PA to Editor
Basic Function: To assist Editor with the co-ordination of her work and department.

Main Responsibilities

1 Organising Editor's diary and appointments.
2 Having a thorough knowledge of editorial objectives and priorities.
3 Following through the Editor's initiatives.
4 Ensuring that all correspondence and enquiries have been processed and actioned where necessary.
5 Taking dictation and typing of memos/letters/reports/copy.
6 Circulating information as instructed by Editor.
7 Co-ordination and planning of all inter-departmental meetings.
8 Co-ordinating and arranging special functions.
9 Responsible for supervising the editorial office.
10 Making UK and overseas travel arrangements for Editor.
11 Co-ordinating editorial photographic trips.
12 Helping to co-ordinate travel pages.
13 Researching and keeping information for special projects.
14 Ensuring confidentiality where important.
15 On a monthly basis arranging payments for published readers' letters.
16 When required, representing the Editor at press receptions, travel functions and product launches.
17 Setting up organisational charts, forward planners.
18 Continual update of files, documents and schedules.
19 To be conversant with company policies.
20 To assist in the implementation of the company's health and safety provisions.

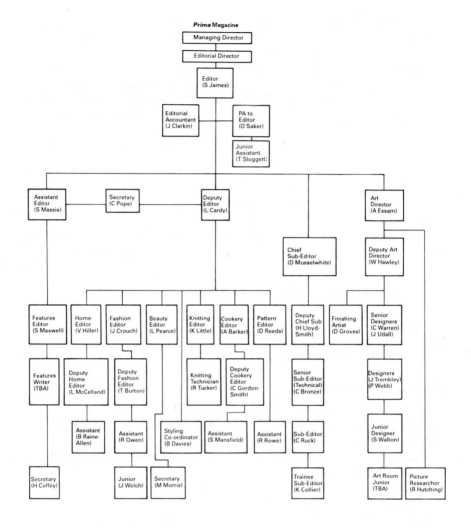

Prima Magazine

Portland House
Stag Place, London SW1E 5AU
Telephone: 01-245 8700
Telefax: 01-630 5509

12 August 19-

Miss Lesley Partridge
18 Crossways
Dublin 1
Ireland

Dear Miss Partridge

Many thanks for your letter regarding our travel article
on Kenya. I'm so glad you enjoyed reading all about the
Safari. Our fashion department went on a photographic
trip to Kenya and had a wonderful time there. It's a
real holiday of a lifetime.

The travel company we used, African Tours and Hotels,
were extremely helpful. They can be contacted at their
Sales Office, 30 Old Bond Street, London W1X 3AD.
Telephone number: 01-491 7431.

I do hope you manage to visit Kenya, and if so we would
love to hear how you got on.

Yours sincerely

Dee Saker
P.A. to Editor

prima is published monthly by Gruner + Jahr (U.K.)

WHAT WOULD YOU SAY?

SECRETARIAL PROCEDURES

17.1 How would you make the Editor's appointments when she has her diary with her? If Sue James made an appointment whilst she was out of the office and it clashed with one you had made for her, what would you do? How could you avoid this happening in future?

17.2 Prepare an itinerary for the Editor to attend the Paris Fashion Collections and to meet influential publishers there. What other arrangements would you need to make for her visit?

17.3 Explain how you would deal with the problem of the late arrival of the camera to ensure that the Editor received it before she left the country.

17.4 How would you (*a*) 'ensure confidentiality where important' and (*b*) 'assist in the implementation of the company's health and safety provisions' as contained in Dee's job description?

STRUCTURE OF BUSINESS

17.5 What factors would the Accountant take into account when deciding the price to charge for the magazine?

17.6 Write an article for the magazine concerning the problems of inflation and unemployment in the UK. Say why we should worry about these problems and what methods can be used to tackle them.

17.7 To what extent is advertising the key to successful marketing of a magazine?

17.8 A reader writes to *Prima* for advice on starting her own business. Draft a letter explaining the various agencies providing assistance and say in what ways the government can help.

SECRETARIAL ADMINISTRATION

17.9 As PA to the Editor explain, with reasons, which of the items in the Editor's mailbag you would: (*a*) deal with yourself; (*b*) pass on to other staff for action; and (*c*) give to the Editor for her attention.

17.10 You are required to organise *Prima*'s Second Birthday Party and make it different from the First Party. Draw up a checklist of the arrangements you would make.

17.11 *Prima* intends to introduce a staff appraisal scheme in the near future. Who should be involved in arranging it? What procedures would you recommend and what benefits would *Prima* gain from the scheme?

17.12 Write an article for the magazine on the changing role of the secretary in today's 'new tech' business world.

MANAGEMENT APPRECIATION

17.13 A future edition of *Prima* includes an article on 'Fair play... and pay for women ... equality at work'. What would you expect the writer to say?

17.14 If the degree of motivation is to be sufficient to give job satisfaction at *Prima* to every member of staff, what basic rules should be followed?

17.15 How would you advise the Editor of *Prima* with a staff of 40 to treat people as individuals, consult with them, communicate with them and set them targets?

17.16 (*a*) Discuss the ways in which *Prima* would use circulation statistics. (*b*) Calculate the percentage of *Prima* readers in relation to the total of women in the UK for each half-year and use them in a bar graph. (*c*) Comment on the trend shown.

ADDITIONAL STUDENT LEARNING ACTIVITIES

FIND OUT

about desktop publishing
- what it will do
- who supplies it
- what it costs
- how it would benefit *Prima*

ROLE PLAY

a planning meeting with your colleagues to make arrangements for a photographic trip to Venice.

Peter Green – household and contract furnishers

INTRODUCTION

Peter Green is a family retail business with seventy employees operating as a private company and built up on the strength of 30 years of experience, personal service and fair dealing. The business is registered under the name of Eastsleep Ltd but trades by the name of Peter Green. The firm specialises in retailing household goods (carpets, furniture, bedding, curtains and fabrics, and vinyl floor coverings) and contract work for furnishing show-houses, offices, shops, factories, hospitals, etc.

Background

The business, which has become one of the largest independent household furnishers in the South of England, was started in 1956 when Peter Green, with the assistance of his wife Norah, opened a small shop in the town of Eastleigh selling bedding. They were very successful and soon had to acquire larger premises to cope with the expansion of trade. A private company was formed with Peter Green as Chairman and Managing Director. Unfortunately, in 1976 plans were announced for a huge covered shopping centre in Eastleigh and the Peter Green site was earmarked for compulsory requisition by the local council. Peter Green felt that it was not viable to operate such a giant business from a shopping centre and, after eight years of uncertainty, a suitable building was found on an industrial estate at nearby Chandlers Ford. The new premises were ideal, offering a total floor area of 37 000 square feet with ample parking space. Sadly, Peter Green died in 1980 before this move was accomplished, Norah took over as the Company's Chairman and Mr Tim Maguire, who had been Peter Green's General Manager since 1967, was appointed Managing Director.

Company objectives

Mr Maguire believes that competitive prices and a personal and reliable service to customers are of paramount importance in a progressive business. Customers are invited to wander freely round the showroom to inspect the goods on display and, if time permits, relax with refreshments in the coffee

Peter Green's showroom.

bar. The sales staff are instructed not to approach customers unless they ask for service, but advice is freely given when requested. Peter Green also offers its customers a professional interior design service with advice on total furnishing schemes. The policy of the company is to offer goods at keen prices by keeping expenses as low as possible and to back this up with a reliable after-sales service – their motto is, 'Peter Green is not satisfied until you are'.

Current developments

The firm's latest innovation in selling lines, which is proving very popular, is 'The Scandinavian Studio' which offers customers a quality collection of

Danish designed and manufactured furniture (with up to 2 years' free credit with Mercantile Credit Co. Ltd). This line is arranged through the Danish Furniture Marketing Bureau who provide a link with the Danish manufacturers contributing to the 'Scandinavian Studio' scheme. Furniture brochures are produced by the Bureau and overprinted with Peter Green's details.

In addition to importing furniture from Denmark, Mr Maguire has been successful in exporting goods from his warehouse. to several European countries, the Gulf and West Africa. He has also recently furnished houses in the Falklands as a result of an introduction by the Falkland Island Development Company. The goods are packed in cases and sent abroad by local shipping agents.

ORGANISATION OF THE COMPANY

An organisation chart is provided on page 151. The principal functions of the senior management team are as follows:

Managing Director

Co-ordinates the work of all departments but deals directly with:

- Marketing, sales and publicity
- Public relations
- Personnel (recruitment, employment, training and staff appraisal)
- Safety
- Security

Financial Director and Company Secretary

- Financial administration
- Office administration, including use of computer
- Company secretarial functions: legal requirements, board meetings, insurance, etc
- Transport – drivers, etc

Merchandising Director

- Buying and supervision of stock

Contracts Manager

- Administration of the Contracts Division

Communication and training

The Managing Director chairs management meetings which are held regularly and staff training meetings take place at the commencement of business on

Saturday mornings (generally a slack period for trade). Training covers such areas as customer relations, safety and security procedures, new product knowledge and sales administration (mark up, profit margins, etc). Mr Maguire adopts an 'open door' policy of communication with his employees and also meets staff regularly at their workplace when he 'walks the floor'.

All offices and stores are linked by a modern telephone system and staff can be located and messages relayed from the switchboard by means of a tannoy. Telex has not so far been used but the company is currently considering whether to install fax, principally to place orders with suppliers, although it might also prove beneficial in receiving orders for contracts from firms. On investigation, Mr Maguire discovered that less than half of their existing suppliers were accessible by fax and this factor would have a bearing on his decision.

Computerisation

The purchase ledger, payment of invoices, salaries and cost records have been computerised, but the sales ledger is still compiled manually as most orders are paid for in cash at the time of delivery. Sales documentation is controlled simply by NCR handwritten, multi-coloured form sales dockets for orders in excess of £5 (*see* specimen form on page 150). The forms are used for the following purposes:

- white copy – for arranging fitting and/or delivery
- pink copy – for use by accounts section in compiling accounts records
- yellow copy – for customer's receipt
- green copy – departmental file record

A word processor is used for the preparation of interior design proposals but it is not used extensively by other departments.

Stationery supplies are ordered and stocks maintained and controlled by the Chief Cashier.

SECRETARY'S ROLE

Mrs Vera Mould, the Managing Director's Secretary, provides the major secretarial service for the company, carrying out typing tasks for all departments except Contracts and Interior Design. Vera previously worked as a secretary in the motor trade and in the construction industry before joining Peter Green 13 years ago. She uses an electric typewriter, preferring it to the more modern electronic typewriters. Her responsibilities include:

- Shorthand-typing for correspondence
- Typing quotations, agenda and minutes of meetings
- Opening and despatching the post – postage stamps are used in preference to a franking machine as the purchase of a machine is considered an unnecessary expense

- Filing – using vertical filing cabinets and alphabetical classification by customers' and manufacturers' names, and by subject for other matters
- Telephone enquiries
- Making appointments for the Managing Director
- Copying correspondence on an office copier which works well but has none of the modern facilities for reduction, enlargement, etc

In organising her work Vera gives priority to the Managing Director's work, although she is expected to type quotations on the day they are received. She does not use audio-typing and considers that shorthand is far superior and more reliable, with her notebook providing a permanent record of dictated material and a point of reference which is invaluable if a document is mislaid.

As with her employer, Vera makes regular contact with the staff and is able to assist with their welfare and lend a sympathetic ear to any of their problems.

CONTRACTS OFFICE ADMINISTRATION

Mrs Marion Bateman is responsible for the office administration of contracts placed with the firm from a customer making an enquiry, say, for a house to be carpeted, to the receipt of the cheque. This procedure entails the following stages:

1 Receipt of enquiry by telephone or letter
2 Arrangements made for estimator to visit the premises
3 Estimate typed and despatched
4 Order received and entered in order book
5 Goods requisitioned from the warehouse or manufacturer and fitter's visit arranged
6 Invoice typed and despatched
7 Statement typed and despatched
8 If payment is not received after 28 days, a final demand is sent
9 Cheque received, entered in records and passed to Cashier for payment into the bank

Marion is well known by most of her customers and she establishes a cordial and friendly relationship with them. This personifies the 'family business' spirit which is reflected in the personal relationships of staff at all levels of the firm and the manner in which the staff are motivated to maintain a highly successful business enterprise.

SCHOOL LANE, CHANDLERS FORD
EASTLEIGH, HAMPSHIRE SO5 3DG
Tel.: CHANDLERS FORD 269011
VAT Reg. No. 188 5507 23
Eastsleep Ltd. Reg. in London No. 601532

Name	Mr and Mrs A.B. Jones,
Address	13, Pilchards Road, Eastleigh

Delivery Address/ Instructions		Date Delivery/ Fitting	Sat 28 OCT

Sold by	Initial Payment	Balance	Customers telephone no.		
M		COD	Work	Home 7643	

Office Use Only	Items	Description			
	1	Marianne Three Piece Suite			
		2 Sear Sofa			
		Wing Chair, Ladies Chair			
		Cover : Malibu		699	00
		Invoice Payment made			
		by Barclaycard			

	Total Price	699 00
Received by Date 25 / 10 / 88	Initial Payment	199 00
	Balance	500 00

C 10340

Prices inclusive of VAT unless shown as addition to total. This bill must accompany all claims and returned goods.

E. & O. E.
Thank you

SR 105567

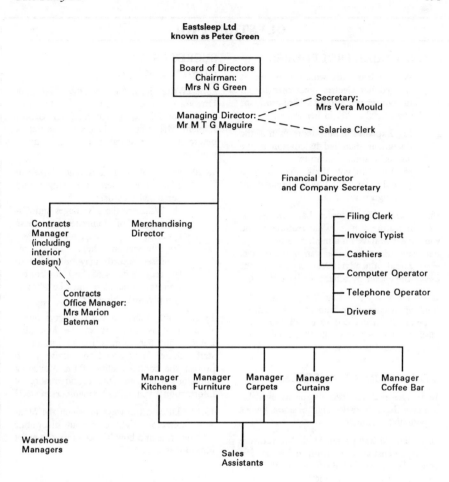

**Eastsleep Ltd
known as Peter Green**

Board of Directors
Chairman:
Mrs N G Green

Managing Director:
Mr M T G Maguire

Secretary:
Mrs Vera Mould

Salaries Clerk

Financial Director
and Company Secretary

Contracts
Manager
(including
interior
design)

Merchandising
Director

Filing Clerk

Invoice Typist

Cashiers

Computer Operator

Telephone Operator

Drivers

Contracts
Office Manager:
Mrs Marion
Bateman

Manager
Kitchens

Manager
Furniture

Manager
Carpets

Manager
Curtains

Manager
Coffee Bar

Warehouse
Managers

Sales
Assistants

QUESTION PAGE

SECRETARIAL PROCEDURES

18.1 What advantages would there be if Vera changed her electric typewriter for an electronic typewriter? Would a word processor also be beneficial to her in her work?

18.2 (a) Explain the purpose of each of the documents handled by Marion in the administration of contracts.

(b) Why do you think Vera was expected to treat the typing of quotations as a high priority task?

18.3 Vera's office copier has few of the modern features on it. What features would you expect to have on a modern copier? Excessive use of a copier can be expensive. How would you advise Vera to control the use of the copier by other members of staff?

18.4 Do you agree that the purchase of a franking machine is an 'unnecessary expense'? If Peter Green decided to install a franking machine, what action would they need to take before it could be used?

STRUCTURE OF BUSINESS

18.5 Describe the various means available to Peter Green to make their business known to potential customers.

18.6 The 'Scandinavian Studio' furniture is offered to customers with up to 2 years' free credit. What are the advantages to the seller and the buyer of this method of deferred payment and how does it differ from hire purchase?

18.7 (a) Explain the importance of the terms 'mark up' and 'profit margins' used in the training of sales assistants.

(b) What advice would you give to sales assistants on the acceptance of cheque cards and credit cards?

18.8 Explain:

(a) How Peter Green has been assisted and constrained by local and central government and

(b) How Peter Green affects the economy of the country.

SECRETARIAL ADMINISTRATION

18.9 Write a memo to the Managing Director in support of your case for the introduction of fax equipment at Peter Green. Explain what steps would need to be taken before and after installation of the equipment.

18.10 (a) Would you advise Peter Green to computerise their sales ledger and personnel records?

(b) What are the advantages and disadvantages of computerising these systems?

(c) Information held on computerised records may be subject to the requirements of the Data Protection Act. What steps must be taken to comply with this Act?

18.11 Could there be any conflict between Vera's role as Secretary to the Managing Director and her informal role of assisting in staff welfare? How would you advise her to protect the confidentiality of the Managing Director's work and the confidentiality of information given to her by members of staff?

18.12 Discuss the ways in which the Managing Director might carry out his public relations role and how his secretary can assist him in this work.

MANAGEMENT APPRECIATION

18.13 Discuss the factors which Peter Green would have to take into account when they were selecting a new location for the firm.

18.14 Comment on the methods of communication used in the Peter Green Organisation and explain the purposes of Mr Maguire's 'open door' policy and 'walking the floor'.

18.15 Mr Maguire has outlined his objectives for the firm as a whole. What objectives would you suggest should be set for:

(a) his Secretary;

(b) the Finance Director and Company Secretary;

(c) the Merchandising Director?

18.16 Prepare a report for the Managing Director outlining the advantages to be gained from creating a new post of Personnel Manager at Peter Green and attach a suggested job specification for the post.

ADDITIONAL STUDENT LEARNING ACTIVITIES

FIND OUT

- what are NCR forms
- what documents are required to export goods to the Falklands
- why estimates are used by the Contracts Department and quotations by other departments

ROLE PLAY

a sales representative visiting Peter Green to demonstrate to Vera the advantages of using audio-typing equipment for correspondence and Vera's arguments in favour of shorthand.

Southampton City Council

BACKGROUND TO THE CITY

'Working for You' is the theme of Southampton's City Council and the visitor is very conscious of this when entering the Civic Centre. The City Council employs some 2200 people, 1500 of whom are engaged in administrative and professional work.

Southampton – an area of 4900 hectares with a population of more than 200 000 – is a vibrant and enterprising city where many national and international companies have their headquarters. It is one of the largest office centres in the south east outside London. Southampton is widely considered to be the South Coast's leading shopping centre and has many major department stores as well as a wide range of specialist shops.

Southampton's world-famous port is the principal economic generator not only for the city but the surrounding area too. Approximately 10 000 people are employed in the port by the many shipping companies and by the factories on the industrial estate. The operation of the port is closely linked with many industrial and commercial undertakings in and around the city and it is estimated that 30 000 jobs in the Southampton area are concerned with port-related activities.

COUNCIL COMMITTEES

The Council, composed of all elected members, is the supreme policy-making body, but the volume of business necessitates delegation of decision-making through a framework of committees and sub-committees, each responsible for particular areas of services. Each full committee has fifteen members, with political groupings broadly represented in a similar proportion to their membership of the full Council. Much of the Council's power is delegated to these committees and for day-to-day working purposes they are autonomous in many matters, but issues of major importance or those involving expenditure of substantial sums of money must be referred by the committees to the full Council for approval.

The Policy and Resources Committee is responsible for determining the authority's overall priorities and policies; co-ordinating the activities of the

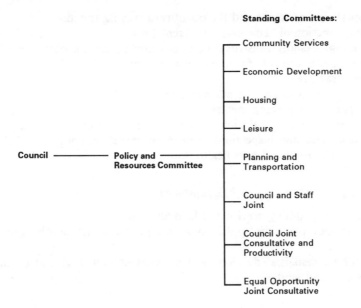

The Committee structure

service committees; the overall financial policy; approving the revenue budget and capital programme and recommending the rate levy to the full Council.

ORGANISATIONAL STRUCTURE OF THE COUNCIL

The organisational structure of the Council (*see* the organisation chart on page 165) is based on directorates, each headed by a Director who is required to advise the Council on policies within their area of responsibility. Their functions are as follows:

Chief Executive

- Co-ordinating and directing the activities of the Council's employees
- Public relations
- Economic development

Director of Technical Services

- Design, management and supervision of new building and the adaptation of existing buildings
- Implementation of building control and administration of housing improvement grants

- Property maintenance and the quantity surveying function
- Client function of cemeteries and crematoria
- Planning, design, construction, improvement and maintenance of highways, sewers and other civil engineering works
- Land drainage
- Street lighting and traffic management
- Car parks and parking meters
- Food inspection and hygiene, occupational health enforcement, pollution control, housing inspection, control of pests, nuisances, disinfection, health education and port health duties

Directorate of Planning and Development

- Integrated planning service and land allocation
- Determines planning applications and produces the Southampton City Plan
- Acquires, manages, develops and disposes of industrial and commercial property and land

Directorate of Law and Administration

- Secretarial, legal and ceremonial services
- Printing and stationery supplies
- Registration of land charges
- Elections
- Archives

Directorate of Personnel and Management Services

- Recruitment
- Employment
- Training
- Industrial relations
- Management services

Directorate of Works

- Manages the direct labour organisation which undertakes work in building, highways, sewers and public lighting
- Street cleaning, refuse collection and public toilets
- Works vehicle fleet
- Engineering maintenance operations

Directorate of Leisure, Tourism and Amenities

- Art gallery, museums, archaeology, and other cultural activities
- Parks and swimming pools
- Catering and recreation

- Entertainment Centres and Public Halls
- Promotes and develops tourism
- Allotments
- Community development services
- Promoting conferences
- Special events, including the annual Southampton Show, Balloon Festival, etc

Directorate of Finance

- Supervises and controls the income and expenditure of the City, advising on financial policy
- Financial accounting
- Internal auditing
- Computing services
- Collects rates
- Pays salaries, wages and pensions
- Central purchasing and supplies service

Directorate of Housing Services

- Council houses
- Housing assistance to the private sector
- Housing advice centres

Personnel and Management Services

Traditionally, the personnel and management services role has been based on centralised control and prescriptive national agreements. With the development of the commercial approach (competitive tendering for services, etc) and greater local flexibility in matters such as conditions of service, the emerging need is for the personnel function to be more concerned with strategic management and the achievement of corporate goals. These new concerns involve the personnel management process; human resource management; supporting Directorates with specialist and technical advice; advising the Directors' management team and Council; and safeguarding the well-being of employees. Wendy Gardiner is the Training Assistant within the Personnel and Management Directorate and assists the Training Officer to provide a wide range of training and staff development support services.

SECRETARIES IN LOCAL GOVERNMENT

This case study describes the roles and experiences of seven secretaries/ personal assistants employed by the Southampton City Council with varying lengths of service from six weeks to 20 years.

The Southampton City Council secretaries at one of their workstations.

Maggie Cotter

Maggie is Audio Secretary to the Assistant Director (Valuation Services) in the Planning and Development Directorate. She has worked in this office as a typist/word processing operator for over six years and was promoted to her present position six months ago. She began her career in local government when she left school, but left it for a few years to become a professional ice skater and later a show skater, which gave her an opportunity to travel abroad.

Maggie provides a personal secretarial service for the Assistant Director. A major part of her work is concerned with the typing and preparation of committee reports. These are supplied to her by means of audio dictation and manuscripts and contain:

1 Report Number
2 Security status, eg Confidential
3 Main headings: name of committee, date of meeting and directorate's name
4 Subject heading
5 Recommendations
6 Introductory paragraph
7 Body of report with relevant headings
8 Conclusions

Maggie uses a word processor for all her typing needs and prefers to deal with all confidential matters herself. She is responsible for supervising three audio-typists/word processing operators, who provide a typing service for the

Valuation Services and Property Management Divisions. She allocates their work, monitors their output and carries out any training required in word processing. Maggie has established a good relationship with her staff, who work well as a team, but on one occasion she was required to deal with a problem arising from a complaint about one of her staff who had used the office telephone for a lengthy private call to a friend.

The Assistant Director has asked Maggie to look into ways of modernising and refurbishing the offices in order to create a new image, and to prepare a report for him. She has to consider the floor covering, curtains, decoration and furniture for a suite of ten offices. Another division of the authority has recently been refurbished and it was suggested that she should look at it, as well as seeking the views of staff in the various offices. She is conscious of the need to consider the possible requirements of new technology which will be introduced in the future.

Marina Doglio

Marina is a new recruit to local government, having joined the authority only six weeks ago on a temporary contract to undertake the work of the Secretary/Personal Assistant to the Director of Planning and Development whilst she is on maternity leave. Her main duties involve typing correspondence, dealing with telephone calls and visitors, filing and organising meetings, lunches, etc. The filing is organised centrally in the Planning and Development Directorate and a filing clerk is responsible for filing much of the correspondence, but Marina keeps files within her own office for each of the committees attended by the Director and for confidential personnel matters. She uses a word processor but, as the printer is housed in another office and shared by other typists, delays can occur in obtaining copies. As a new secretary at the Civic Centre Marina has experienced some difficulty in determining work priorities and in knowing which matters her Director would wish to see and which can be re-directed to others. Some people are very persistent in their desire to speak to the Director and a great deal of tact and diplomacy is needed to satisfy 'awkward' people on the telephone or when they call at the office.

Marina has had an interesting and varied career. She was trained as a medical secretary and worked in this capacity for four years, leaving it to spend a year in the USA with 'Camp America'. She returned to England to work at the Head Office of B & Q as Secretary to the Marketing Development Controller until she took up her present position six weeks ago. She likes working in organisations which provide personal services to the community, such as hospitals and local government, in preference to business profit-making concerns. In her work as a medical secretary she was associated with the Departments of Oncology and Psychiatry which entailed typing reports on patients, arranging clinics and making appointments, and recording the results of tests and examinations on medical records. She was in regular contact with patients, some of whom were unwell and in a distressed condition.

Sheila Harris

The longest-serving member of the secretarial staff interviewed, Sheila has worked in local government throughout the whole of her career. She is Secretary to the Director of Finance, a position she has occupied for the last ten years. This involves:

- filtering and re-directing correspondence and other communications to appropriate staff in the Directorate
- drafting replies to correspondence, eg replying to an invitation addressed to the Director to an open day of a play group which receives a grant from the Council
- assisting in the arrangement of management, inter-directorate and Councillor meetings
- receiving and providing hospitality for guests and officers as required
- preparing for meetings and taking minutes
- maintaining the filing system for the Director

The present Director of Finance was appointed to the position a year ago, following the retirement of the previous Director and, as a result, Sheila's role and responsibilities changed. She now has a more varied job and greater opportunities to use her initiative.

Sheila is responsible for three secretarial staff (the Secretary to the Assistant Directors and two word processing operators). There is at present a vacancy for one of the word processing posts and she has prepared the advertisement and job description for it. When the replies are received she will select a shortlist of applicants for interview and take part in the interviews. She would like to employ someone with the following skills and qualities:

- fast and accurate typist (a copy-typing test containing figure work will be given at the interview)
- proven ability in audio-typing and word processing
- ability to think and use initiative
- correct spelling
- neat appearance
- capable of working well within a small team

Much of Sheila's work relates to Officer Meetings on various topics. She keeps a separate file for each meeting and, before giving it to the Director, she checks that it is up to date, with the minutes of the last meeting inserted. Sheila is responsible for organising the weekly Finance Management Team Meetings and this entails assembling items for the agenda; typing and distributing the agenda to the senior management team; arranging refreshments; and typing minutes from handwritten notes. These notes are recorded by one of the group leaders, who each attends in turn to give them an insight and training in policy-making strategies.

The Director of Finance is the Chairman of the Joint Geothermal Project Team. Southampton is the UK pioneer in using geothermal energy for heating. Water naturally heated by the planet's hot interior is being vigorously pumped to the surface from more than a mile below the city, and used for heating. The Civic Centre and nearby Marlands House are the first buildings in the country to be heated by this unusual source of alternative energy – power which will help to supplement the earth's rapidly-depleting conventional energy sources.

Sheila has a part to play in this important project by arranging the monthly meetings of the Project Team and she had responsibility for organising the press launch on 13 July 1988 when over 100 members of the press, guests, contractors, engineering consultants, Department of Energy Officials, etc. were invited. She prepared the programme for the day; distributed invitations; organised refreshments; arranged transport to take the visitors to view the works; and typed name badges.

Most of the word processing facilities at the Civic Centre operate from a minicomputer with distributed terminals but it will soon need to be replaced with more up-to-date equipment. Stand-alone microcomputers have proved to be very effective in some of the offices and they may be used to replace the older equipment. Sheila is of the opinion that, with the use of word processing facilities, some staff are inclined to be less precise in drafting correspondence, knowing that amendments can be incorporated by text processing. As a result, the typists spend more of their time making amendments and producing revisions. In her long career in local government Sheila has witnessed many changes since her early days as a shorthand-typist and, although admitting that she does not know how her career will develop, she is obviously prepared to adapt to whatever changing role and techniques are required of her.

Janette Horswell

Before taking up her present position as Secretary/Personal Assistant to the Director of Leisure, Tourism and Amenities seven years ago, Janette had gained varied secretarial experience with estate agents, solicitors and a firm of wholesalers/importers. Her present position involves:

- Filtering and re-directing correspondence to staff for action, and drafting replies to correspondence
- Arranging meetings, preparing agenda and recording and typing minutes
- Typing correspondence and supervision of the support secretarial staff
- Telephone communications – Janette receives many telephone calls from members of the public wishing to speak to the Director and she has to determine whether he should be interrupted to deal with them. It is not always possible or desirable for a caller to be connected to him and in these circumstances Janette listens very carefully to the caller's request and if it is not possible for her to give the information requested or to re-direct the call to someone who can deal with it, she agrees to ring the caller back after making the necessary enquiries
- Making appointments and keeping the Director's diary
- Keeping up to date with the general work of the Directorate to enable her to liaise with colleagues on behalf of the Director and take messages, queries, etc, in his absence, obtain the necessary information and/or request action as required – an information unit is operated from the city's

central shopping precinct which is supplied with all details of the Directorate's activities
- Maintaining a comprehensive filing system

The Conference Unit of the Directorate provides the following services to
assist organisations holding conferences in the city:

- liaises with local hotels and if required makes bookings
- arranges for the booking of halls
- arranges catering facilities
- supplies conference packs for delegates with information about the city
  and its facilities
- with the assistance of the Public Relations Department, certain conferences are offered a civic reception with the Mayor in attendance

At the time when this case study was compiled the Director had been away
from the office for eight weeks as a result of an illness. At first Janette
arranged for urgent mail to be sent to his home but as the period of the
illness was prolonged she ceased to do this and arranged for his deputy to
attend to his business.

Janette is involved in organising a variety of interesting events. For
example, she served as Secretary to the Organising Committee of the Tall
Ships Race, arranging meetings and liaising with the Public Relations
Department, the Docks Board and the College of Nautical Studies. She was
also the Appeals Secretary of the Wessex Heart Fellowship (an organisation
with which the Director was actively involved) and in this capacity she
helped to organise various fund-raising events.

Kim Hunt

Kim has been Secretary/Administrative Assistant to the Head of Project
Services in the Directorate of Technical Services for the past nine months.
Before this she was engaged as Personal Secretary to the Pensions Marketing
Executive of a national insurance company after working as a Cashier/
Administrator with a building society.

Kim's duties in her present post involve typing correspondence from
manuscript and shorthand; keeping the Head's diary and arranging appointments, meetings and seminars; dealing with telephone enquiries; filing and
ensuring that matters are followed up when required; collating and preparing
information required for meetings, taking notes at meetings and preparing a
record of decisions taken; dealing with administrative procedures for the
recruitment, selection and appointment of staff for three divisions of the
Directorate; keeping records relating to leave and sickness and assisting with
other administrative tasks for the division concerning project planning and
quantity surveying. She also has some supervisory responsibilities for a word
processor operator/clerk and part-time clerical assistant. On one occasion a
problem arose when the Division's Administrative Assistant was called away
urgently and no-one knew how to do her work. Certain essential tasks had to
be done during her absence and Kim managed these with some difficulty,
referring to the procedure manual for guidance and also coping with the

pressures of her own job. Arrangements have since been made to ensure that this situation does not occur again by allocating a cover rota for the division's administrative tasks involving Kim, the Administrative Assistant, the Clerical Assistant and WP Operator/Clerk.

At the beginning of each day Kim prepares a list of tasks to be completed in order of priority. She has to decide, for example, which of the following tasks are high priority to be undertaken urgently and which are of a lower priority and can, if necessary, wait for attention:

(a) Contacting Councillors concerning a date for a meeting.
(b) Informing the Head of Division of a staff problem.
(c) Typing correspondence for the Head of Project Services.
(d) Filing yesterday's correspondence.
(e) Arranging interviews for new staff.
(f) Despatching application forms to applicants for a vacancy.
(g) Reorganising the filing system.
(h) Requisitioning stationery supplies.
(i) Processing car allowance claim forms.

Kim has recently been appointed training co-ordinator for the Project Services Division and in this capacity is responsible for disseminating information about courses to staff and arranging for them to attend approved courses. During the last year Kim has attended a five-day course entitled 'Women into Management' which interested her and gave her assistance in managing her present position, especially with time management, dealing with priorities, and delegation of work.

Maureen Queen

Maureen has been in her present position as Secretary/Personal Assistant to the Head of Engineering in the Technical Services Directorate for nine months. In her spare time she serves as a Parish Councillor which allows her to experience local government at two levels. She had previously occupied various secretarial positions in engineering and yacht building companies, as well as working as a 'temp' with a staff agency. Maureen considers the variety of experience gained from 'temping' to be good preparation for a top-level secretarial career.

In her present position Maureen maintains that one of her more important tasks is to make sure that the Head of Engineering attends his meetings at the right place, at the right time and with the right information. She also has a key role as communications/liaison resource, ensuring that the cross-flow of information runs smoothly. She is responsible for the Head's secretarial services involving correspondence, diary, appointments, meetings, telephone calls, visitors and filing. She monitors important letters received from Councillors, Members of Parliament, Residents' Associations, etc, to ensure that action is taken as quickly as possible. These are recorded in an incoming mail book which contains a number for each letter; date received; name of correspondent; subject matter; file number; name of person required to deal with the letter, and the date of the reply letter.

When she first took up this post Maureen found that the office filing cabinets were full and difficult to manage with a considerable number of the papers 5/6 years old. She soon remedied the situation by devising a file retention policy and applying it to the system to thin out the files. Records of council business are computerised in a database and can be accessed on the computer terminals.

Maureen attends a working party of divisional secretaries with the object of standardising the layout and style of correspondence used throughout the Directorate. It is proposed to produce a sample pack of correspondence for the information of all secretaries. Maureen welcomes opportunities to use her initiative and particularly enjoyed the task of devising an age profile of staff in the division to assess the percentages of staff in each age group. In order to further her career prospects in local government Maureen has enrolled on a day-release course at the local college for the Higher National Certificate in Public Administration.

Susan Watson

Susan joined the Southampton City Council a year ago to become Secretary to the Assistant Director (Central Division) of the Directorate of Technical Services. She had previously worked in secretarial positions at British Teleflower, Gresham Computer Services and the Hambleside Group Ltd. In her present position Susan is responsible for the full range of personal secretarial services to the Assistant Director. She organises the weekly Management Meetings of the Division, preparing agenda, taking notes at meetings and writing the minutes. She considers that the most important elements of her job are co-ordinating matters for the Assistant Director and being his 'memory jogger' for action to be taken, meetings to be attended, etc. She also regards her responsibility for shielding him from unnecessary callers to be important as it prevents him from being disturbed too frequently, although he insists that if staff have a problem they should be given immediate access to him. Susan has to decide which of the following callers should be put through to the Assistant Director:

(a) The Director of Technical Services
(b) A technical clerk requesting unpaid leave
(c) A Councillor
(d) A representative of a firm selling parking meters
(e) A NALGO Representative
(f) His wife
(g) Secretary to the Chief Executive wishing to discuss available dates for a meeting
(h) A member of staff wishing to discuss a grievance.

Susan recalls the occasion when she received a telephone call from the Car Park Attendant to say that the Assistant Director had arrived but could not get out of his car. He had been stricken with a severe back complaint and could not move. He was eventually eased from the driving seat and driven home and was away from the office for three weeks. Susan was left to take such action as was necessary on the day of the accident and for the period of the illness.

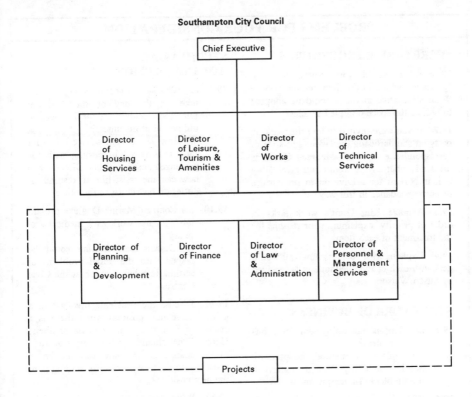

Southampton City Council

Chief Executive

| Director of Housing Services | Director of Leisure, Tourism & Amenities | Director of Works | Director of Technical Services |

| Director of Planning & Development | Director of Finance | Director of Law & Administration | Director of Personnel & Management Services |

Projects

PROBLEMS FOR YOUR CONSIDERATION

SECRETARIAL PROCEDURES

19.1 What would you expect Maureen Queen to include in the file retention policy? What alternative methods could be adopted to reduce the space occupied by files?

19.2 If you were invited to join the working party on standardising the layout and style of correspondence in which Maureen Queen is involved, what advice would you give? Why is it important for a Division to standardise its correspondence in this way?

19.3 Arrange Kim Hunt's work tasks in order of priority, explaining your reasons for the treatment of each item.

19.4 Explain, with reasons, how you would deal with each of the telephone calls received by Susan Watson.

STRUCTURE OF BUSINESS

19.5 (a) Why is unemployment an economic problem?
(b) Explain the methods adopted by Southampton City Council to alleviate the problem of unemployment.

19.6 What do you understand by 'the development of the commercial approach in local government (competitive tendering for services, etc.)'? What arguments can you put forward *for* and *against* the privatisation of public services?

19.7 In what ways does local government intervene in business to protect the consumer?

19.8 Outline the structure of your local district council and explain the influence it has on the business community.

SECRETARIAL ADMINISTRATION

19.9 (a) What action should Susan Watson take on the day of the Assistant Director's accident and for the succeeding period of his illness?
(b) How would your advice differ for Janette Horswell in dealing with the prolonged absence of her Director and how can she assist him to resume his duties on his return to the office?

19.10 (a) Contrast Marina Doglio's present job with her work as a medical secretary.
(b) Discuss how Marina could be helped with the initial problems of settling into her new job at the Civic Centre.

19.11 Discuss the problems involved in a private secretarial position when there is a change of Director, as in the case of Sheila Harris. What should the Secretary's attitude to the change be and how can she be of assistance to the new Director in settling in to the new position?

19.12 What changes have been made in the office since Sheila Harris began her career in local government and how do you think her role and techniques will change in the future?

MANAGEMENT APPRECIATION

19.13 A flexitime system for staff working hours operates at Southampton City Council. What are the advantages and disadvantages of this system for the employees and the employer?

19.14 What would you expect Kim Hunt to learn about time management, work priorities and delegation at the 'Women in Management' course? What other topics might be included in such a course?

19.15 Discuss the Director of Finance's initiative in introducing group leaders to the senior management team to give them an insight and training in policy-making strategies. What other management techniques should be included in the training of managers?

19.16 How would you expect Kim Hunt to solve the problem of covering the Administrative Assistant's work when she is absent from the office?

ADDITIONAL STUDENT LEARNING ACTIVITIES

FIND OUT

information for Maggie Cotter on floor covering, curtains, decoration and furniture for refurbishing the suite of ten offices and draft the report required by the Assistant Director.

ROLE PLAY

Maggie Cotter's talk with her member of staff, reprimanding her for using the office telephone for a lengthy private call to a friend.

Jobways Commercial Services

INTRODUCTION

This case study features the career of Karen Irving who built up her own very successful business following a varied and interesting secretarial career. At the conclusion of her grammar school education in Manchester, Karen moved to the south of England and attended a full-time secretarial course at the Eastleigh Technical College. She gained outstanding results in the RSA examinations and was awarded the course prize for her achievements.

SECRETARIAL WORK

Karen started her secretarial career as a shorthand-typist in the Staffing Department at the Regional Hospital Board offices and during the following twelve years gained valuable experience with:

- a major departmental store where she worked as a junior secretary in the staffing department, later to become the Staff Manager's secretary
- a group of doctors where she worked as a medical receptionist
- a consultant dermatologist, running his private practices in Winchester, Salisbury and Harley Street and commuting to London once a fortnight
- a Member of Parliament who was also one of the first British MPs serving at the European Economic Community headquarters in Brussels and Strasbourg
- a property developer for whom she worked as secretary and office administrator

TRANSITION FROM SECRETARY TO BOSS

In 1976 Karen's career took off in a different direction with her ambition to be her own boss and start up her own business. She had always been good at art and thought that she could use this talent to design office stationery, menus, etc. Also, there appeared to be a need in the area for an employment

Karen Irving, proprietor of Jobways Commercial Services.

agency for office staff and, with her wide-ranging secretarial experience and skills, she thought she could make a good business out of taking in typing and duplicating for local firms. So Karen launched her new venture under the title of Jobways Commercial Services.

During her secretarial career she had accumulated some money in the bank which provided the opening capital to buy the essentials – an electric typewriter, a stencil duplicator, filing cabinets, furniture, stationery, and the lease of a small office to begin her business. As a secretary she was familiar with the meticulous planning which has to go into any successful business and was also conscious of the difficulties that she would have to face, such as:

- managing with limited resources
- her lack of knowledge and experience of some aspects of running a business
- the inadequacy of facilities for tackling some of the tasks she could be asked to undertake
- attracting sufficient customers in the first year or two to make the business pay
- the excessive amount of time she would need to devote to the business without the assistance of others
- manning the office telephone throughout the day and the cost of employing staff to relieve her of this task

Business Plan

In drawing up the plans for her business Karen took into account such key issues as:

1 The purpose and place of the business in the office services industry

Establish the likely demand for the office services planned. Karen's view was that by offering firms attractively designed stationery and literature and by producing high-quality work she could help them create a favourable impression, communicate effectively and present their firms in the best possible light. She was aware that she would need constantly to review the services offered as a result of her experience.

Consider the likely competition in the office services industry.

2 Production methods

Examine the methods and systems needed, taking account of the essential accommodation and equipment to begin the operation and those required in, say, three years' time.

3 Finance

Determine capital requirements to begin the venture and the operating costs in the first year. Allocate desirable financial ratios, such as return on capital employed and profit margins, and aim to maintain an adequate cash flow. Costing of jobs would have to take into account wages of any staff employed, overheads (premises, equipment, electricity, rates, insurance, etc) and cost of materials. Establish a rate per hour for normal services which would have to be adjusted annually to take account of increasing prices.

4 Marketing

Consider which promotional techniques to use, eg direct mailing, advertisements, personal visits, etc, and determine the annual marketing budget. In the locality there was a new and expanding industrial estate with many small firms and this would be the main marketing target in the first year of operation. The pricing of the services would have a major influence on marketing results.

5 Personnel

Assess the need for the employment of staff – part-time in the first place until the volume of work could be established. Consider the skills/experience required in staff, wages to be paid and methods of recruitment to be used.

6 Administration

Office systems to be set up:

(a) work scheduling
(b) ordering of materials/services
(c) invoicing
(d) stock recording
(e) wages
(f) accounting
(g) filing
(h) mailing

Consider:

Legal requirements
Office layout
Commercial services such as bank, post office, insurance company and accountant.

STARTING AND DEVELOPING THE BUSINESS

Karen leased small office premises, acquired the equipment and started drawing and designing menu cards and letter headings. She spent considerable time visiting hotels, restaurants and small businesses to market her products, but when she was out seeing potential customers there was no-one in the office to answer the telephone, and it was not long before she decided to employ a part-time assistant for a few hours per week and offer a typing and duplicating service to cover these costs. Karen did the artwork herself and sub-contracted the printing. The artwork expanded to such an extent that she also had to take on the services of a part-time artist. It was soon obvious that this should be the main direction of the business and Karen decided to discontinue the employment agency aspect of her work. The other branches were now flourishing and she was taking in substantial amounts of typing and duplicating for local firms. This had increased as a result of a 'mail shot' targeted at the nearby industrial estate. When following up enquiries in the industrial estate she realised that there was no up-to-date street map available so she decided to draw and print one and use it to publicise Jobways' services. She operated as a sole trader and has continued to remain in business on her own.

Over the next few years the work continued to expand and Karen took on full-time as well as part-time staff. She was already short of accommodation and rented two more rooms and updated her equipment by purchasing memory typewriters for text storage at a time when word processing was just evolving. A Christmas card service was provided for firms where Karen supplied the cards and arranged for the necessary printing and this proved to be popular and profitable. She established close relationships with printers and because of the volume of business now handled she could expect keen terms with them. Another interesting development was that Jobways were approached by the local Chamber of Commerce to provide a 'hot line' or telephone answering service for them at a time when their secretary was not available to receive calls during business hours.

Jobways moved to new premises some eight years ago and at the same time installed a large Xerox copier for the fast production of prints, specialising in multi-page originals.

The business today

Jobways employs a full-time staff of five people together with a further three part-time assistants (*see* the organisation chart on page 174). Regular customer contact and job satisfaction coupled with job variety in pleasant surroundings have attracted a good team of staff. Karen takes a personal interest in each member of her staff and reviews their salaries annually. A professional accountant is engaged to produce the final accounts and tax returns. A college leaver has recently joined the firm to assist with general office duties and to learn the print/design side of the business. Karen had no difficulty in identifying the qualities and skills she required in applicants for this post. She looked for a person who was 'word conscious' with a sound command of the English language to be able to correct English errors in manuscripts; a reliable proof-reader; a competent typist with good display skills and a steady, conscientious person able to work well in a small team.

Communications are essential in an organisation dealing with a diversity of activities: daily informal staff meetings take place to co-ordinate the work and to discuss requirements for the following day's work schedule. One of the major problems of running a small business is coping with the peaks and troughs of work and meeting the often tight deadlines set by customers. Another problem is dealing with the many office equipment representatives who call at the office to convince Karen of the need to buy the latest office machines and equipment.

The office now has one of the large Xerox copiers which is capable of printing 1000 copies in 10 minutes and has automatic collation, reduction facilities and a computer forms feature. There is a back-up copier which uses colour cartridges. Karen is considering the possibility of acquiring one of the latest copiers with full colour facilities as there is an increasing demand for coloured copies. They have the necessary electrical binding equipment to prepare comb-bound technical reports, house journals and manuals. The artist has a daylight camera for producing bromides for artwork. The typists continue to use the memory typewriters but it is likely that replacement word processors will be introduced in the near future. Computerisation of the office procedures is another development which it is hoped to bring about as soon as possible, as well as the possibility of doing desktop publishing. Although a franking machine has been considered for the mail, as the post office is situated on the ground floor of the office block, there is no difficulty in purchasing postage stamps when required. Karen has adopted the policy of leasing expensive items of equipment to avoid the problem of possessing 'white elephants' when they become obsolete.

A mailing list in excess of 300 customers, mainly firms, is maintained on index cards and the services offered to them include:

- Copying: letters, price-lists, manuals, booklets, newsletters, advertising material, etc
- Over-printing: letter headings
- Artwork: designing and printing letter headings and all kinds of promotional stationery, including forms, brochures, invitation cards, programmes, menus, etc, as illustrated on page 175

A large amount of work is now undertaken for garden centres, producing their price-lists, circulars and leaflets.

A system has been set up to encourage customers to pay their bills promptly in order to provide a regular income and a satisfactory cash flow situation. The office systems incorporate the completion of government returns such as VAT, income tax and national insurance. Invoices for the work tasks are typed and sent out when the jobs are completed and statements are issued to the regular 'credit' customers once a month. Filing of correspondence is arranged alphabetically by customers' names and the job cards, used to record costing details and progress of tasks, are filed numerically by job number.

Karen attaches great importance to serving the needs of her customers in an efficient and personal manner. The experience she gained in different secretarial capacities has helped her to run a successful business. She has been able to bring to it her secretarial skills, organising abilities and presentation skills which she considers essential for a business specialising in office services and the production of professionally printed material.

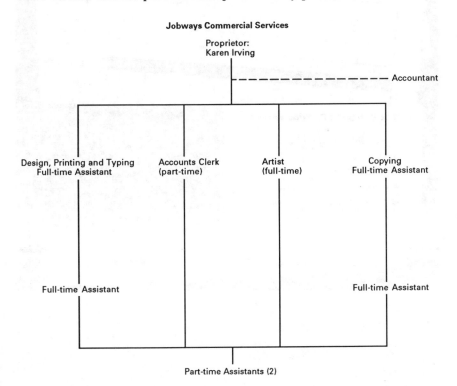

AND NOW FOR YOUR OPINIONS

SECRETARIAL PROCEDURES

20.1 What documents would Karen need to use when she began to employ staff? What is the purpose of each of these documents?

20.2 How would you advise Karen concerning the layout of her offices? What equipment and materials would she require when she started her business?

20.3 Would Jobways benefit from using a franking machine? If they decided to purchase one, what action would be necessary before it could be used?

20.4 How could Karen solve the problem of manning the telephone without employing staff? Would your proposal affect her desire to serve her customers in an efficient and personal manner?

STRUCTURE OF BUSINESS

20.5 What different business units would be used by the employers of Karen's secretarial positions and how would each of them be financed?

20.6 What are the advantages enjoyed by Karen as a sole trader and what benefits could she expect by going into a partnership with others or by forming a private limited company?

20.7 Jobways provided a telephone answering service for the local Chamber of Commerce. What questions are the business community likely to ask of this service and how would Jobways benefit from joining the Chamber of Commerce?

20.8 Karen leases expensive items of equipment. Discuss the advantages and disadvantages of this policy and compare leasing with other methods of acquiring equipment.

SECRETARIAL ADMINISTRATION

20.9 Explain the different roles which Karen performed during her secretarial career. Suggest a reference book for each of the positions which would assist her in her work.

20.10 What benefits could Jobways expect to gain from the computerisation of their office procedures? What steps should Karen take to determine the feasibility of this development?

20.11 What is desktop publishing? How would Jobways benefit if they acquired it?

20.12 Discuss modern methods of reprography. Would you advise Karen to acquire a copier with full colour facilities?

MANAGEMENT APPRECIATION

20.13 How would Karen's role as proprietor differ from her role as secretary?

20.14 Discuss an idea you have for setting up your own business and prepare an outline business plan which you would need for it.

20.15 Discuss Karen's objectives for her business in the office services industry (page 170). How would they differ if she had developed the employment agency business?

20.16 How would you solve the problem of the 'peaks and troughs' of work in a small business?

ADDITIONAL STUDENT LEARNING ACTIVITIES

FIND OUT

what sources of advice and assistance are available when you are planning to start your own business.

ROLE PLAY

an interview with the bank manager to persuade the bank that you have a good idea for starting your own business and that you should be given a loan.

Comparisons and conclusions

SECRETARIAL PROCEDURES AND ADMINISTRATION

21.1 What reference books or other sources would you use to find out more about each of the organisations in the case studies?

21.2 State three documents which are in common use at each of the organisations and say how they could be filed.

21.3 Name a meeting which takes place at each of the organisations and in each case say what it is intended to achieve.

21.4 Give an example of the use made of new technology in each of the organisations.

21.5 Identify three secretarial positions depicted in the case studies which appeal to you and would give you most satisfaction, giving the reasons for your choice.

21.6 Compare the role and functions of a secretary in:

(*a*) one of the large organisations with one of the small organisations;
(*b*) a manufacturing industry with a service industry.

21.7 Suggest how a database might be used in three of the organisations.

21.8 Which of the organisations have introduced electronic mail? What are the current limitations to the extension of this facility?

21.9 Name four centralised office services and identify the organisations in which they are to be found.

21.10 Explain the importance of public relations in four of the organisations.

21.11 Compare the information storage and retrieval systems used in four of the organisations.

21.12 Say what you understand by:

(*a*) a secretarial will (case study 6); (*c*) a performance plan (case study 6);
(*b*) secretarial back-up   (*d*) EFTPOS (case study 10).
    (case study 7);

STRUCTURE OF BUSINESS

21.13 List the twenty organisations under the following categories:

(*a*) Profit-making organisations (manufacturing/trading);

(*b*) Profit-making organisations (services);

(*c*) Non-profit-making organisations.

21.14 List each of the organisations under the following business unit categories. Explain briefly how these business units differ.

(*a*) sole trader   (*d*) public limited company

(*b*) partnership   (*e*) public undertaking.

(*c*) private limited company

21.15 In which of the organisations are the following people employed?

Management Adviser; Head of Visual Services; Taxation Partner; Production Editor; Operations Manager; Director of Strategic Operations; Legal Executive; House Exchange Controller; Warehouse Manager; Merchandising Manager.

21.16 What are the major sources of income for each of the organisations?

21.17 Which of the organisations could have an effect on the country's balance of payments?

21.18 State an item of statistical data kept in each of the organisations and say how it would be used.

MANAGEMENT APPRECIATION

21.19 State two examples of each of the following relationships contained in the case studies:

(*a*) line relationships;   (*c*) staff relationships;

(*b*) functional relationships;   (*d*) lateral relationships.

Say how these relationships differ.

21.20 Compare the role and style of management in one of the large organisations with those in one of the small organisations.

21.21 Define the principal objectives for each of the organisations.

21.22 Compare the different methods of recruitment, selection and training of staff used in the case study organisations.

21.23 Name the principal Acts of Parliament relating to office administration and say how they affect particular organisations given in the case studies.

21.24 Say what you understand by:

(*a*) interpersonal skills (case study 4);

(*b*) quality circles (case study 4);

(*c*) open door policy (case study 6);

(*d*) accountability chart (case study 7);

(*e*) delegation (case study 7);

(*f*) cost effectiveness (case study 10);

(*g*) time management (case study 11);

(*h*) non-executive directors (case study 15).

Index of topics in the activities

	case studies																			
	1	2	3	4	5	6	7	8	9	10	11	12	13	14	15	16	17	18	19	20
Accountancy	x								x											
Advertisement – job												x								
Advertising			x											x		x	x			
Aims for organisation														x						
Alcohol						x														
Appointments				x	x												x			
Appraisal interviews							x													
Audio-typing																		x		
Authority		x																		
Auto pay system					x															
Balance of payments		x		x										x						
Balance sheets	x														x					
Bank clearing system							x													
Bank, employment in										x										
Bank lending rate									x											
Bank of England										x										
Bank personal services										x										
Bank services							x			x										
Books of reference		x							x					x		x				x
Budgeting			x										x							
Business documents					x									x			x			
Business plan																				x
Business units																				x
Capital, sources of										x										
Cash flow					x															
Central government					x				x		x			x			x			
Centralisation	x		x																	

	case studies																			
	1	2	3	4	5	6	7	8	9	10	11	12	13	14	15	16	17	18	19	20
Chamber of Commerce	x																			x
Collation of documents												x								
Communication methods	x		x	x		x	x						x	x			x	x		
Community relations						x														
Company products															x					
Company structures				x																
Computer communications																x				
Computerisation of records		x	x	x	x								x	x				x		x
Conference planning		x																		
Confidentiality								x					x	x		x		x		
Consultation with staff																	x			
Consumer protection																			x	
Copiers																	x			
Cost effective methods										x										
Cost of living													x							
Cover for staff									x											
Data Protection Act 1984		x																	x	
Debt collection				x																
Delegation	x	x					x				x		x						x	
Departmental functions		x	x																	
Design			x																	
Desktop publishing																	x			x
Development			x																	
Diary								x								x				
Dictation, audio										x						x				
Dictation of reports and correspondence							x													
Directors – functions															x					
Dismissal of staff					x															
Diversification															x					
Electronic funds transfer										x										
Electronic mail				x																
Electronic telephone						x														
Electronic typewriter																		x		
Employment law												x								

case studies	1	2	3	4	5	6	7	8	9	10	11	12	13	14	15	16	17	18	19	20
Employment of staff					x					x						x				x
Employment of women						x														
Estimating prices						x														
European Community (EC)						x							x							
Export trade											x							x		
Family business								x												
Fax	x															x	x			
Filing			x					x			x	x			x			x		
Finance – sources										x										
Financial Services Act										x										
Flexitime																			x	
Follow-up system						x		x												
Form design					x										x					
Forms of address														x						
Franking machine																		x		x
Functional relationships	x																			
Furnishing offices																			x	
Goals for achievement											x						x			
Government departments			x										x							
Graphs and charts		x															x			
Health and safety	x																x			
Health services												x								
Hospital administration												x								
Hostess duties							x						x							
House exchange plan									x											
Induction course		x												x	x				x	
Industrial relations			x	x			x	x												
Industry, importance of							x													
Inflation																		x		
Initiative, use of		x							x		x		x				x			
Insurance						x			x		x	x								
International trade											x									
Interpersonal skills				x							x									
Interview, organisation of									x											
Interview selection					x										x					
Itinerary													x				x			

	case studies 1	2	3	4	5	6	7	8	9	10	11	12	13	14	15	16	17	18	19	20
Job description					x	x	x		x			x								
Job sharing								x												
Job specification					x				x									x		
Layout of offices																				x
Leadership				x																
Leasing equipment																				x
Letters, standard										x										
Line relationships	x								x											
Local government					x	x			x					x				x	x	
Mail – incoming					x							x								
Mail – outgoing					x							x								
Management functions														x						
Management philosophy																x				
Management problem-solving techniques		x																		
Management styles										x						x				
Management techniques												x							x	
Management theorists			x																	
Management training															x					
Managing Director				x																
Marketing							x				x					x	x			
Marketing mix															x					
Marketing research				x																
Maternity provisions									x											
Medical secretary																			x	
Meetings	x			x		x				x	x		x			x	x			
Memory aids		x																		
Microfiche												x			x					
Minutes of meetings		x							x											
Motivation								x				x			x		x			
Multi-national company						x														
Nationalisation															x					
Network planning													x							
New post, preparation for									x											
New technology						x				x		x		x						
Objectives of business														x				x		x

case studies

	1	2	3	4	5	6	7	8	9	10	11	12	13	14	15	16	17	18	19	20
Office equipment/ materials																				x
Organisational changes											x									
Organisation and Methods												x		x						
Organisation charts		x							x											
Organising a car rally														x						
Organising a conference							x													
Organising a lecture			x																	
Organising a lunch/dinner							x		x											
Organising a party															x		x			
Organising a visit											x		x				x			
Overseas agents			x																	
Overseas trade									x											
Overtime				x																
Partnerships	x				x			x												
Payments, methods of													x					x		
Performance plan						x														
Personnel functions/role	x							x										x		
Personnel policies and procedures							x				x									
Person profile											x									
Petty cash													x							
Pie chart											x									
Planning				x																
Policy-making strategies																			x	
Press relations		x												x						
Press release														x						
Prices, calculation of																	x	x		
Printers' correction signs			x																	
Priorities for work			x					x								x		x		
Private limited company					x	x										x				
Privatisation of services																			x	
Proprietor, role of																				x
Public corporations		x																		
Publicity																		x		

case studies

	1	2	3	4	5	6	7	8	9	10	11	12	13	14	15	16	17	18	19	20
Public limited company						x									x	x				
Public relations	x		x			x				x		x		x				x		
Quality circles				x		x														
Record cards													x							
Recruitment of staff			x						x	x						x				
Redundancy provisions											x									
Relationships								x				x								
Relationships with manager						x														
Relocation of premises											x							x		
Reprographic equipment																				x
Research			x																	
Retail trade																x				
Sales financial data analysis											x									
Sales promotion																x				
Secretarial co-ordination							x				x									
Secretarial will						x														
Secretary's duties/role/ qualities	x	x		x		x	x	x		x				x			x	x	x	x
Security				x		x	x									x				
Selection of staff			x							x										
Sex equality																	x			
Shareholders				x																
Shorthand																		x		
Sole trader								x												x
Solicitor's role								x												
Sources of information				x		x				x										
Sponsorship																x				
Staff appraisal	x	x														x				
Staff relationships	x	x																		
Staff/Student handbook													x	x						
Standardisation of documents																			x	
Starting your own business																x				x
Stationery supplies					x						x									
Statistics, use of													x	x		x				
Stock control													x							

case studies

	1	2	3	4	5	6	7	8	9	10	11	12	13	14	15	16	17	18	19	20
Stock exchange										x										
Supervision	x							x			x								x	
Technology industry						x														
Telephone answering machine																				x
Telephone services													x							
Telephone technique					x			x	x										x	
Telex	x																			
Terms of payment																		x		
Time management										x	x		x						x	
Tourist industry														x						
Trade Unions			x																	
Training courses		x				x									x	x				
Training – functions		x	x											x						*
Training organisations						x														
Training programme					x															
Training records		x																		
Travel arrangements		x			x						x					x	x			
Technical and Vocational Education (TVE)						x														
Turnover					x															
Typing authors' manuscripts			x																	
Typing services							x									x				
Unemployment												x					x		x	
University												x								
Viewdata				x																
Visual planning charts		x	x									x								
Wages					x															x
Welfare																		x		
Wholesale trade																x				
Women in management																		x		
Word processors			x		x			x		x					x	x		x	x	
Work scheduling												x							x	x